PASS IT ON

PASS IT ON

WORK HARD, SERVE OTHERS ... REPEAT

DESHAUN WATSON

with LAVAILLE LAVETTE

W PUBLISHING GROUP

AN IMPRINT OF THOMAS NELSON

Pass It On

Published in Nashville, Tennessee, by W Publishing, an imprint of Thomas Nelson, in association with One Street Books.

Thomas Nelson titles may be purchased in bulk for educational, business, fund-raising, or sales promotional use. For information, please e-mail SpecialMarkets@ ThomasNelson.com.

Any Internet addresses, phone numbers, or company or product information printed in this book are offered as a resource and are not intended in any way to be or to imply an endorsement by Thomas Nelson, nor does Thomas Nelson vouch for the existence, content, or services of these sites, phone numbers, companies, or products beyond the life of this book.

ISBN 978-0-7852-3209-4 (eBook)

Library of Congress Control Number: 2020937450

ISBN 978-0-7852-3204-9 (HC)

Printed in the United States of America

20 21 22 23 24   LSC   10 9 8 7 6 5 4 3 2 1

This book is dedicated to my mother,
Deann Watson, and my Watson family.
You are my ROCK, and I love you dearly.

CONTENTS

FOREWORD

Several years ago, I said that any NFL team that passed on Deshaun Watson in the draft would be like turning down a chance to draft Michael Jordan.

I meant that then and I mean it now, more than ever.

That's not just a matter of physical skills. Deshaun and Jordan both have natural ability to spare.

In comparing Deshaun to Jordan, I was also referring to more than athleticism. Having coached Deshaun for several years at Clemson University and knowing him for even longer, I realized what a privilege I had in working with a young man whose dedication and commitment to preparation are at a level that very few athletes achieve.

But it's more than just work ethic. By how he presents himself and goes about constantly improving his play, Deshaun naturally inspires those around him to work just as hard and with the same strength of commitment. He just makes everyone around him that much better.

Phrased another way, his focus on servant leadership—leading through service to others—by both action and example is both natural and inspiring.

The torn ACL he suffered in a game against Georgia Tech illustrates the courage that his leadership embodies. We were scheduled to play in-state rival South Carolina in a couple of weeks, and I thought there was no way Deshaun would be able to play. But Deshaun kept insisting that he would be ready. We rigged up a brace for him and, in practice a few days before the Carolina game, you'd have never known he was hurt.

Going into the game, I gave him strict instructions. Get rid of the ball quickly. If you have to scramble, just go down. Don't get hit.

On our first drive, we were at the Carolina 11-yard line. Deshaun drops back, starts scrambling, and the next thing you know, he plants his foot in the ground and dives into the end zone as he's getting hit. I'm thinking, *Oh my, he's done.* But he just pops up and comes jogging down the field like he's out for a leisurely run.

I remember saying, "This guy is unbelievable." It was obvious to me that Deshaun's dedication, grit, and determination are unmatched.

At my press conference after the South Carolina game, I expressed my joy in snapping a long losing streak against South Carolina, then added: "I just witnessed one of the most amazing things I've ever seen."

I then told a stunned press corps that Deshaun had played the entire game with a torn ACL.

Deshaun's leadership is not only a great example for others; he also has a natural ability to draw others closer to him.

It reminds me of the story that I heard about Deshaun's first day with the Houston Texans prior to the draft. He sat down in the cafeteria to have lunch. Almost immediately, other players began to join him at the same table. It was almost as though they were drawn to him. They recognized that this was a player and a person worth getting to know and learning from.

And with this book, you're getting the same opportunity to come to understand this very special young man and how you can apply what he has learned in your own life.

As you'll read, Deshaun's life was far from easy—growing up in a single-parent home in a neighborhood scarred by crime, his mother's cancer diagnosis and struggle to recover, and the series of injuries from which he has always managed to rebound.

Overcoming those and many other challenges has only served to strengthen Deshaun's character and approach to everything he does. I think that's because he understands the value of learning from every experience. No matter if it's winning a national championship or rallying his family in the face of his mother's illness, Deshaun's ability to find something of value in both the good and the bad has helped make him the man he is.

That's how he's become such a remarkable servant leader. He doesn't just give orders by being of service to others in times of crisis or challenge—he inspires confidence, hard work, and a sense of belonging to something greater than yourself. That's the best kind of leader you could ask for.

In *Pass It On*, Deshaun repeatedly returns to the importance of servant leadership, whether on the football field or through helping others struggling to get by in the wake of tragedy. The setting really doesn't matter. In taking advantage of every opportunity to serve others, he knows that you don't merely offer someone else a helping hand—in doing so, your character, faith, and humanity benefit as well.

That's one of the reasons why, in recruiting Deshaun to Clemson University, I gave him my word that we would build the program around him. As I got to know him both as a player and a person, I realized his emotional strength and sense of obligation to others mandated nothing less.

I like to say that Deshaun is the same guy, day in and day out. What you saw yesterday, you'll see again today and tomorrow. And as you read this book, I know you, too, will recognize how his values and commitment to service never waver.

Pass It On offers a close-up look at a remarkable young man whose rise to the top of the athletic world has every bit as much to do with character built through service to others as it does with athleticism. As you read this book, you'll come across a number of important and helpful ideas, including:

1. The value of resilience.
2. Recognizing when it's "not your time."
3. Failure is the best teacher.
4. Forgive the haters.

With those and other thoughts to look forward to, I'm genuinely excited about all that Deshaun has to pass on to you.

—Dabo Swinney,
Head Football Coach, Clemson University

ACKNOWLEDGMENTS

This book would not be possible without the love and support of my mother, Deanne Watson, my Auntie Sonia, and my Watson family.

A very special thank-you to David Mulugheta, Bryan Burney, and Quincy Avery—you are the heart and soul of my team on and off the field.

So many individuals have helped me along my journey: Mrs. Maria Herbst, my Clemson advisor; high school coaches Michael Perry, Tyler Perry, and head coach Bruce Miller; Clemson head coach Dabo Sweeney, Chad Morris, Clemson offensive coordinator, and all of the coaches and staff at Clemson University; Jack Waldrip, Violet Waldrip, and Andy Miller, my mentors in Gainesville; pastors Michael Thurmond and Jenson Franklin. And thank you to the entire Houston Texans organization.

To the publishing team at HarperCollins, W Publishing Group, and One Street Books, thank you for your hard work and dedication: Lavaille Lavette, Jeff Wuorio, Dawn Hollomon, Damon Reiss, Sara Broun, Alex Woods, and Matt Baugher.

Last but not least, my gratitude extends to all those individuals, corporations, and organizations that have contributed to my efforts to *Pass It On*.

INTRODUCTION

It was time.

I stepped into the greenish water and walked until it came up to my chest. My white T-shirt clung to me, and I had to strain to hear the words of the rabbi over the wind that rushed past. He explained what would happen next. I nodded and took a deep breath. I was ready.

I had encountered many life-defining moments before—a football state championship in high school, a national championship in college. Watching my mother face down cancer. But this wasn't just another experience. I knew, even as I stood there in that cold water, that this moment was more important.

The rabbi stepped forward, put his arms around me, and leaned me back. I pinched my nose as he lowered me into the Jordan River. The cold water closed over me, and then I was lifted up again. I couldn't believe it. I had just been baptized in the homeland of my faith.

My baptism in Israel was the highlight of a life-changing visit to the Holy Land in 2019. I have always treasured the lessons history can teach us, and I was completely captured by the stories of both the land and the people of Israel during my time there. I absolutely loved standing on the banks of the Jordan River, looking out at the site where the tabernacle stood after Joshua led God's people into the promised land. Trying to take it all in, I was humbled and overwhelmed but also felt a strong sense of peace and reverence all around me.

I knew how lucky I was to be there. I could never have imagined standing in this place when I was a boy growing up in rural Georgia with no father and a mother who struggled to afford to keep her family fed. I also knew that I wanted to encourage other people to chase their dreams, just as I had, and to see how far those dreams could take them. I hoped that my being in Israel would inspire those who started out like I did to be able to see themselves there—or wherever their version of this dream was—someday too.

As a quarterback in the National Football League, I've learned that when you're an athlete, particularly a professional one, a lot of people are looking at you. And they're not looking at you just on the playing field, although success in my craft has always been something I value enormously. I am constantly in the public view. When you're a quarterback, people look to you to be a leader of your team, whether you want to be or not. That's just part of the position. You're the one calling the shots, you're the one all your teammates look to on the field, and you're seen as the team's representative off the field as well. My role, I've come to understand, is bigger than throwing a football.

MY ROLE, I'VE COME TO UNDERSTAND, IS BIGGER THAN THROWING A FOOTBALL.

I didn't start playing quarterback because I wanted to be in charge. It's just the position I felt the most excitement about, and the one that felt the most natural to me, ever since I first took the field in high school. But with that role, I quickly realized, came expectations. Because I was the quarterback, people looked to me to lead, even back when I was a scrawny freshman. Those expectations only grew once I got to Clemson University and then into the NFL.

So I decided that if I was going to be seen as a leader, I wanted to do it intentionally. I didn't want to just lead by default—I wanted my decisions to inspire and motivate people to want to do great things. I wanted to lead with meaning and purpose and never let anyone down.

Once I set my mind on something, I am totally dedicated to making it happen. As you'll learn, I've been exposed to some remarkable leaders, people with the energy, commitment, and focus to bring out the best in everyone around them. I thought about the leadership they gave me, and I began to look for a common point, something they all expressed in their leadership style.

I discovered there were far more leadership styles than I had known about. There were leaders who sought input on every decision, while others were more autocratic. Some were involved in everything having to do with the groups they led, while others were hands-off.

Still I noticed common threads. All the leaders I admired commanded respect. They didn't have to demand it—it was their due. From my tutor in college to the various coaches I've been blessed to work with, respect was a given. Further, none of those leaders simply barked orders. Rather, they showed me why one particular idea or strategy would work and how I could best use it. Just as important, in leading this way, they truly wanted to make me better at whatever I was doing. That really resonated with me.

I remember a conversation I had with a friend when I was a rookie in the NFL. At some point, the topic of leadership had come up. She'd mentioned that my style of leadership wasn't particularly forceful, nor did I ask everyone around for their opinions while making a decision.

Instead, she said, my demeanor was closer to that of a servant leader—someone who looks to serve those around him or her first, then turns their attention to leading. Unlike other leaders for whom leadership itself is the top priority, a servant leader emphasizes service above everything else. That appealed to me a great deal.

The term *servant leader* attracts a lot of buzz, but I can't help but think that many people don't understand what it truly means. The phrase was coined by Robert K. Greenleaf, founder of the Greenleaf Center for Servant Leadership. Greenleaf was a business and management executive who studied leadership for a number of years and determined that many leaders were ineffective in their roles. Rather than focusing on their own power and authority, leaders were far more influential when they served the people they were charged with leading. Servant leaders put the needs of those they're leading before their own. They make sure the people they're leading are experiencing growth. They think of others before themselves.

I embraced those ideals in part because they represented the same sort of leadership I saw in how Jesus interacted with his disciples back in the days when he was walking alongside the Jordan River. That was the kind of leadership I wanted to model: effective, powerful, and sacrificial.

One of the qualities of servant leaders is that they inspire others around them to follow their own dreams, and that's where this book comes in. In this book I will lay out the eleven rules, or guiding principles, I try to live by. My hope is that these principles will inspire you to go after your dreams too.

Why eleven? There are eleven players on each side of a football game—it seemed like a natural way to arrange things! These principles are:

Never Forget Where You Came From: Always embrace your past because that's what helped make you the person you are today. Your roots help you identify not only the need for leadership in particular situations but also what you have inside you to offer to others—how you can be of service to them to help them grow and succeed.

Focus on What You Have, Not What You Don't Have: Sometimes it takes the struggles of others to put into perspective all that you should truly be grateful for.

Prepare for Success: If you want to win, you have to put in the work. If you have to ask yourself if you're sufficiently prepared, the answer is no.

Your Word Is Your Oath: When you make a commitment, you stand by your word.

Failure: The Best Teacher There Is: Winning is wonderful, but losing can teach you so much more.

Never Get Too High, Never Sink Too Low: Balance is key.

Ignore the Doubters, Forgive the Haters: Stay focused and positive, no matter the negatives swirling around you.

Bend, Don't Break: Palm trees that bend survive storms, while other more rigid trees don't. Follow the palm trees' lead.

Never Stop Practicing, Never Stop Learning: Stay a committed student.

Stay Humble: Perspective is everything.

Find a Coach, Be a Coach: Once you've gained knowledge from a great coach, pass it on to someone else.

I'll expand on these principles using stories and experiences from my life—from my childhood through high school, college, and, ultimately, professional sports. Although my goal is to share ideas and lessons that can be applied to anyone's life, there will be plenty of football stories for fans eager to get an inside view of what happens at the highest levels of the sport. Football has been much too important in my life not to tell some entertaining stories that also underscore my journey as a servant leader.

I feel very strongly that if you apply these principles consistently in your life, you will not only succeed in whatever dreams you may pursue but also share that strength and success with everyone else you come into contact with.

Each chapter will include information to help you "Pass It On," with questions and suggestions that will guide you to develop or further refine those characteristics and attributes of servant leadership. Lastly, I'll end with a specific challenge that will give you tools and encouragement to make a difference in someone else's life.

At the end of the book I've included stories for the die-hard football fans—personal recaps of games that meant a great deal to me. Additionally, I've added an imaginary game of sorts: my perfect game, which to me embodies not only great competition but also valuable leadership lessons.

Dream big, achieve big—that's one of the core messages I want you to take away from this book. As you'll learn, I was able to graduate college in just three years (two and a half, as I like to say if I'm being really specific), and, as I write this, I am truly living the dream of being a starting NFL quarterback for the Houston Texans. If I can do those sorts of things, there's no reason in the world you can't also do whatever you truly desire to accomplish. Anything is possible.

That said, the journey won't always be easy. Everyone experiences hurdles and setbacks. In my case, I've suffered significant injuries that came very close to completely derailing my football career. Some thought I was finished. But time, faith, and determination have seen me through, as I'm sure they will again with the next change or obstacle I face.

A servant leader anticipates that challenges and problems are going to occur. Those are a fact of life, no matter the circumstances. When you expect them, you can be that much better prepared to meet them and deal with them in a thoughtful, constructive manner. In fact, it's valuable to look at failure as more than just disappointments or setbacks. That's because failure is a far better teacher than success. You always learn more from losing. Through adversity, I have learned how to improve at my craft and be a better leader when confronted with challenges. I've also learned how not to be complacent (a topic I'll get into more later).

TIME, FAITH, AND DETERMINATION HAVE SEEN ME THROUGH, AS I'M SURE THEY WILL AGAIN WITH THE NEXT CHANGE OR OBSTACLE I FACE.

I hope there's something in this book that will inspire everyone. In particular, though, I hope young readers will benefit from my stories and observations. Although I firmly believe this book can benefit people from all walks of life, I feel strongly about setting an example for young people who are just beginning their own journeys. Opportunity is everywhere for them, and in sharing my story, I hope to illuminate that truth in a powerful way. With commitment, faith, and an open heart, most anything is possible. I'm living proof of that.

I know some people may wonder how someone in his mid-twenties has sufficient experience and insight to write a book about being a leader. Well, for one thing, I readily admit I don't know everything. On the other hand, I have both the willingness and an eagerness to continue to learn. You'll see as I share stories throughout, I have been fortunate to have learned from remarkable people and circumstances—on the football field, at home, in the classroom, in different countries, and most everywhere else. And I am determined to continue to learn in all areas of my life, personal and professional.

WITH COMMITMENT, FAITH, AND AN OPEN HEART, MOST ANYTHING IS POSSIBLE. I'M LIVING PROOF OF THAT.

We all lead in one way or another, and I want to help you make the most of your opportunities. Go out and be a leader—in your family, community, vocation, or wherever your life takes you.

MY COMMITMENT TO HUSTLE, TO CONTINUE GRINDING WHEN I WANT TO QUIT, AND MY TOUGHNESS WERE DEVELOPED AS A RESULT OF THE CHALLENGING CONDITIONS I ENCOUNTERED EVERY DAY.

CHAPTER 1

NEVER FORGET WHERE YOU CAME FROM

Football has always been a way for me to escape. No matter the level of play—from pickup games on cement to the bright lights of the NFL—I've found refuge in the game I love. And every time my team won a game, other realities dimmed, at least for a little while.

When I was a kid, I really needed that escape. I could lose myself in the plays and the strategy of the game, imagining I was throwing the winning pass in the last seconds of the Super Bowl. Fantasies like this helped me get through the stuff I had to deal with every day.

I grew up in Gainesville, Georgia, about seventy miles from Atlanta.

The city's primary enterprise is the poultry business, so much so that Gainesville labels itself the Poultry Capital of the World. Unfortunately, the prominence of the poultry business did little to alleviate the widespread hardship throughout the city. Many of the families that lived there amassed household incomes that fell below the poverty line, and often well below it.

We were one of those families. For much of my childhood, we lived in a government housing complex called Harrison Square. It was dismal, made up of one- and two-story brick buildings. Many of them had been built in the 1970s and showed their age: railings were rotting, the brick was chipped. Residents strung up clotheslines everywhere. No one had a clothes dryer.

I was one of four kids, the second oldest. I have an older brother, Detrick, and a younger brother and sister who are twins, Tinisha and Tyreke.

I never knew my father. I've met him a few times—perhaps five at most. His name is Don Richardson. As long as I can remember, he seemed set on staying out of our lives.

My mother, Deann, juggled a number of jobs trying to keep us all clothed and fed. When she was pregnant with the twins, she enrolled at a technical college in hopes that education and training would make it possible for us to move out of Harrison Square. But with all of us to take care of, there just wasn't time for school.

The reality of living in government housing always intruded— often, very cruelly. Gunfire was never much of a surprise. Street fights were common. We frequently heard our neighbors fighting, screaming, and crying. Domestic violence was pervasive. Gang violence was commonplace in our neighborhood, the natural outcome of precious little hope mixed with a hunger for fast fixes, with little regard for those who might get hurt along the way. Often there was too much danger outside for me to leave the house and play, particularly after the sun went down.

The effects on young people who lived in Harrison Square were the most noticeable. Many became mothers and fathers when they were barely teenagers. Young people were forced into roles and responsibilities well beyond their years. A common saying around the area was that the kids there grew up awfully fast. Since, in many cases, they were pretty much raising themselves, they had no other choice.

What I remember most about my childhood neighborhood was the pervading sense of helplessness. In our eyes, the neighborhood was just one big recycling bin, and no one ever really made it out. You'd be back sooner or later. It seemed to happen to everyone.

There was always something standing in the way for anyone who wanted to get out of the neighborhood. For my mom, the burden of trying to raise a family and keeping them safe and fed overruled continuing school at the technical college. There simply weren't enough hours in the day. For other people, crime might have raised their standard of living a little bit, but it was far from a ticket out. If anything, it cemented their permanency in Harrison Square.

> WHAT I REMEMBER MOST ABOUT MY CHILDHOOD NEIGHBORHOOD WAS THE PERVADING SENSE OF HELPLESSNESS. IN OUR EYES, THE NEIGHBORHOOD WAS JUST ONE BIG RECYCLING BIN, AND NO ONE EVER REALLY MADE IT OUT.

Then there were others who had simply given up. With far too many things stacked against them, they were resigned to staying in Harrison Square. If there was no way to escape, why bother even trying?

My family and friends did what they could to make life in that kind of setting as normal as possible. Like other little kids, I attended school: Centennial Arts Academy. I remember that my prekindergarten graduation included a class presentation of the story of "The Three Little Pigs." I played the Big Bad Wolf. (My childhood friend Brenton Merritt later remarked that it was probably the only time in my life I was cast as the villain.)

I was always good at math but struggled a bit with reading. One thing I didn't struggle with was keeping my desk clean and orderly. While other kids' desks were usually a mess, mine was immaculate, with books, papers, and pencils always orderly. (To this day, I don't like messiness, even when it comes to how my teammates huddle up!)

I was like that at home too. My mom remembers me as a little boy stretched out on our ragged carpet, playing with whatever I could find—plastic men, marbles, or other trinkets. No matter what I was playing with, I always arranged the toys in perfect rows. I moved them with precision. Every piece had to be in a certain spot. There were no exceptions to this sense of order. That may be why I love mapping out football plays to this day. I love the thought it takes, the specifics of the positions, and how one piece relates to the others.

I recall the very moment when I first recognized my love for football. I remember being eight years old and charging toward the convenience store across the street from our Harrison Square apartment. I had done a few chores and errands the prior week and had fifty cents rattling in my pocket. I knew just what I wanted to buy.

I plowed into the store to buy a copy of the local *Gainesville Times* newspaper. After carrying it back home, I promptly tossed away everything but the sports section. I wanted to read about what had happened in high school football across the state.

If I couldn't attend a game in person, I made sure to read about it in detail in the newspaper afterward. In particular, I paid special attention to the offenses—what plays they had run, what players they had used, trying to get a sense of the overall game plan. I'd then try to replicate the games myself with marbles or some other objects carefully arrayed on the floor.

PlayStation was a real revelation for me. When we got the game *NCAA Football*, I made up my own league of more than two dozen imaginary high school teams. Then I took it one step further by creating players for each of those teams. I even went so far as to attach certain habits to particular players, such as the way one guy stretched his hamstrings or carried his helmet on the sidelines.

I sought to make each team as realistic as possible, with both strengths and weaknesses. Some might have had a great defense while struggling on offense. Some might have had a particularly strong passing game, while others relied more on the run. To me, that sense of order mirrored real life.

Unsurprisingly I was a rule follower. I was a little shy, but I always had plenty of friends around me. I would laugh when someone pulled a prank, but I rarely got into any mischief of my own doing. A photo of my fourth grade class captures my childhood pretty well. I'm standing in the back row, a skinny, somewhat tallish kid dressed in a T-shirt and jeans, the hint of a grin spreading across my face.

I spent much of my time playing pickup football and basketball games. There were plenty of basketball courts scattered throughout the neighborhood, and as for football, that could happen anywhere from an open field to the street. Many of the older kids I played with were the drug dealers and gang members who, off the field or court, made our neighborhood the violent, desperate place that it was. In a strange way, we all got along when we were playing sports. They all seemed more human and normal, not people for whom crime was as natural as breathing.

It was one of my first lessons in the importance of trying to see the whole person, not just one aspect of someone's life. A guy whom I'd seen in a fistfight a few days before might be my teammate on the basketball court or football field—a good teammate, one seemingly separated from the violence that filled our neighborhood. Normally, I would have avoided contact with those guys—in the evenings, my mom would often ask who I'd hung out with that particular day—but in the context of sports and teamwork, things were completely different.

Looking back, these pickup games also provided some of my first experiences with servant leadership. Since I was a good player and tall for my age, I quietly assumed the role of leader on the basketball court—mapping out plays, distributing the ball. I embraced it, and I began to look at my leadership in terms of success and failure. If a particular play didn't work, I realized that was due, at least somewhat, to a lack of leadership on my part. At some level, I was beginning to understand that I needed to study and grow in my leadership skills. I wanted to be good at leading.

Then leadership took on new meaning. As I improved in all sports, I started to realize that athletics might be my ticket out of the government housing project. I also thought I might be able to help others who had that same dream. (I'm sure there were very few who didn't hope for just that.)

I was careful not to tell people what I was hoping the promise of sports might hold for me. Lots of other guys had bragged about getting a football or basketball scholarship and never looking back. It never panned out, and those who spoke of the hope of riding sports to a better life faced laughter and derision. Most people recognized just how hopeless those dreams would likely be. So I kept quiet.

> AS I IMPROVED IN ALL SPORTS, I STARTED TO REALIZE THAT ATHLETICS MIGHT BE MY TICKET OUT OF THE GOVERNMENT HOUSING PROJECT.

But that was part of the environment that drove me. That's why it's so important to never forget where you came from. It helps you determine your goals and overcome some of the challenges you face, and it helps you identify what you need to do to succeed—and to help others succeed as well.

Although I was a talented basketball player, to up my game just a bit, I would pretend I was JJ Redick, a guard who played at Duke University when I was in elementary school. In my head, I was always in March Madness, launching shots at the final buzzer for Mike Krzyzewski—the legendary Coach K—at Duke to nail down a national championship. Since I was JJ Redick, I seldom missed any of those key shots. I knew they were good the minute they left my hand. Back then, JJ was *the* guy. He could shoot threes, which is what I liked to do. He was so cool, so focused. He also wore the number four, which, in no small coincidence, has been my number throughout school and the pros. It was my dream to play basketball at Duke for Coach K.

But my early basketball days were about much more than just draining imaginary championship shots. A grade school teacher of mine once told me that she had been watching me and other kids play on the school basketball court. What had struck her the most was my focus on distributing the ball—making passes to others who had a better scoring opportunity than I might have had. Unlike some of the other boys who were only interested in seeing how many points they could rack up, I wanted to involve others as much as possible.

That has stayed with me to this day. As a quarterback, I feel my job revolves around always finding the open man—not the one who can help me accumulate better statistics but the one who's in the best position to help us as a team succeed. In my mind, the most important goal is success, and who is credited for that success is secondary to achieving it. Winning is the objective, not individual glory or praise.

In addition to basketball, I played baseball and attracted some interest from college and pro scouts. I also took part in track, competing in both the high jump and the two-hundred-meter races at the middle school state championships. But if I wasn't playing basketball, I was usually focused on football.

> IN MY MIND, THE MOST IMPORTANT GOAL IS SUCCESS, AND WHO IS CREDITED FOR THAT SUCCESS IS SECONDARY TO ACHIEVING IT.

I would pretend I was Warrick Dunn, the star running back renowned for his breakout ability and open-field running skills, who played for the Atlanta Falcons for much of my childhood. Maybe, I thought, I could end up playing pro football, just like my idol.

I had actual encounters with football players when I was young. When Hurricane Katrina devastated New Orleans, Kendrick Lewis—who, as an adult, has since played with several NFL teams—transferred temporarily to a high school in Gainesville. He would volunteer at the elementary school, and I couldn't stop staring at him in awe. He was everything I wanted to be.

My fourth grade teacher at the time, Leslie Frierson, noticed and took me aside to give me some advice that has stayed with me to this day.

"You could be bigger than him," she told me. "If you get your schoolwork totally under control, you can go and do anything you want to do."

I believed her, and I will always be grateful to her for her vote of confidence in me. I hope to pass that kind of encouragement along to the kids growing up in my old neighborhood today.

———

As I grew older, a number of people around me helped me realize that success in sports without success in the classroom is a dangerous situation. Sure, you could be the best player around and make all this money, but how would you know how to handle it responsibly without an education to guide you to think critically? How would you know how to use your resources to better the lives of those around you? How would you recognize the very special opportunity you had received?

An educated athlete is a far better athlete, person, and leader than someone who has relied only on physical skill.

Even though the community I grew up in was riddled with drugs, crime, and violence, I have to credit my childhood neighborhood for the person I've become. My commitment to hustle, to continue grinding when I want to quit, and my toughness were developed as a result of the challenging conditions I encountered

AS I GREW OLDER, A NUMBER OF PEOPLE AROUND ME HELPED ME REALIZE THAT SUCCESS IN SPORTS WITHOUT SUCCESS IN THE CLASSROOM IS A DANGEROUS SITUATION.

every day. I knew I had to be dedicated if I was ever going to get out of that neighborhood.

That's why every time I go out on the football field, I wear a wristband with the number 815 written on it in large permanent marker. That was our address: 815 Harrison Square. I want to make certain to remember not only where I came from but also the influence that place had on who I've grown into and who I wish to become. Despite the challenges that place required me to overcome—or maybe because of them—I never want to lose my connection to where I came from.

I try to make it back to Gainesville as often as I possibly can. I love the vibe there, the closeness that so many of its residents feel toward one another. I also make a point of getting over to Harrison Square. As I work to develop my leadership qualities, it's essential that I reconnect with what I consider my roots.

Harrison Square hasn't changed all that much. Although there are some new buildings and there have been some repairs made to older structures, it's still pretty much as I remember it. People hang laundry out to dry on the clotheslines, kids run all over the place, and the air is filled with the low-level buzz of a neighborhood going about its day.

As I said earlier, many people living in these government complexes consider them a sort of recycling bin—an environment you may leave temporarily that will inevitably draw you back.

But I know that not everything is completely the same. I'm different. I'm proud to be one of the exceptions to the rule. Through determination, persistence, faith, and a little luck—not to mention the support of family and countless friends and neighbors—I was able to escape the recycling bin that is government housing. I'm proud to be able to show the kids growing up there today that they can achieve their dreams and goals if they believe in them enough to pursue them wholeheartedly. The endeavor most likely will not be easy, and it may take a long time, but dreams can be attained amid even the most challenging of circumstances. I'm living proof of that.

That's why I make such a point to never forget where I came from. It reinforces the pride I feel in having achieved so much and strengthens my determination to aspire toward new goals. At the same time, it makes me want to inspire others to do the same.

THROUGH DETERMINATION, PERSISTENCE, FAITH, AND A LITTLE LUCK—NOT TO MENTION THE SUPPORT OF FAMILY AND COUNTLESS FRIENDS AND NEIGHBORS—I WAS ABLE TO ESCAPE THE RECYCLING BIN THAT IS GOVERNMENT HOUSING.

Never lose sight of your roots or where you grew up. For better or worse, that environment influences much of what you're going to be for the rest of your life. It's up to you to build on the good and eliminate the bad.

PASS IT ON

- Take a minute or two to consider where you came from. What was your childhood like? Your adolescence? What experiences helped shape you into the person you've become? Which experiences were positive, and how can you build on those? By the same token, what part(s) of your early years do you consider unfortunate? Does any aspect of who you are today derive from a negative experience? What can you do to change that?
- How do you keep memories of where you came from fresh in

your mind? A visual reference point is always helpful. In my case, I write down the address of our government project home on a wristband every time I take the field. Is there something similar—a letter, a photograph, or a keepsake—that reminds you of where you started and, just as important, how far you've come?

- When was the last time you went back to the city, town, or neighborhood where you grew up? What was the experience like? What emotions did it bring out in you? Did you feel an ongoing connection to the place, or did you feel utterly removed? Did it seem odd or foreign? If that was your experience, how did it make you feel?

- If you'd rather forget about your past, think about how you might benefit from keeping in mind where you came from. Set aside an hour or two and consider what you say and how you act. What influence does your past have on your behavior and attitude?

YOUR CHALLENGE

If it's possible, plan a trip to the place where you grew up. Try to pay particular attention to those parts you remember, but also notice how the place has changed. Consider the impact the environment had on you. If you have loved ones (particularly children), try to take them along as well so they can share in the experience of reconnecting with your past. It may teach them more about you and help them understand you more completely.

SO MANY PEOPLE PITCHED IN TO HELP
OUR FAMILY OUT IN THOSE YEARS, AND
I WOULDN'T BE WHO I AM WITHOUT
THEIR GENEROSITY. IT WASN'T
JUST THE THINGS THAT THEY SHARED;
THEY GAVE THEIR TIME, WHICH WAS
IN MANY WAYS MORE VALUABLE.

CHAPTER 2

FOCUS ON WHAT YOU HAVE, NOT WHAT YOU DON'T HAVE

My mom has always put our family first—always. In everything she has said and done, her kids have been foremost in her mind. When I was growing up, we didn't have a lot, but we had each other. We always knew that no matter what happened, we were a family, and nothing could ever change that.

Of course, there were plenty of things other kids had that I wanted—new video game systems, the latest Jordan shoes—but we couldn't always have those things. So Mom tried to get us to focus on the things we did have, and that positivity served us all well in the years to follow.

Mom wasn't, however, content to let us stay in a bad situation. She worked hard to give us the best chance she could, and she knew that our family couldn't have much hope for the future if we remained amid the dangers of our neighborhood. She dreamed of having a home where her children could leave their bikes on the porch without expecting them to be stolen and where we kids could play outside after dark without worrying about stray bullets.

That dream began to take shape when I was nine. It started one Halloween when my mom was inspecting my candy before I ate it. She had taken me and my brothers and sister to a church function since my neighborhood, not surprisingly, was considered too unsafe for trick-or-treating. Each year the church invited area residents to come to an in-house Halloween party, complete with bags of goodies. I can't remember what costume I wore that year, but it really didn't matter. The event was always fun, and I walked away with a bag of loot.

Even at a church-run function, though, my mom never let her guard down for an instant. She insisted on looking through the bag of candy to make certain it was safe to eat while I waited impatiently. After all, I was only there for the candy. I'm not ashamed to admit it.

As she was going through the bag, Mom came across a pamphlet for Habitat for Humanity. It explained how we could qualify for safe, affordable housing if Mom committed to volunteering for a certain number of hours.

After she read through the pamphlet, Mom didn't take very long making up her mind. She decided to go for it. After all, we were in government housing—what could be worse?

Mom signed up with the program and worked nearly three hundred hours of community service to qualify for a Habitat house. Each day after she left her nine-to-five job, she'd log a few hours volunteering at a homeless shelter. She took classes on financial management of a home. On weekends she helped build four Habitat homes—hammering nails and hauling wood.

I usually went along with her. I was too young at the time to help with anything complicated, although I did hammer my share of nails and carry a fair amount of lumber around the job site.

But what I came to love—and still do—about Habitat is the teamwork involved. That's not surprising, given my love of sports. It was inspiring to see volunteers from all types of backgrounds coming together for a common goal to help others. This ran counter to much of the vibe around Harrison Square, where survival was foremost on everyone's mind. The Habitat job sites weren't driven by a mentality of every person for him- or herself; people wanted to work together. Their energy and enthusiasm for making things better were infectious.

My own level of excitement grew when I learned that the last of the four houses we were building was to be ours.

One day when we'd framed the walls and could begin to get a sense of how the house would be laid out, I pulled my mom inside and dragged her toward the middle of three bedrooms.

BUT WHAT I CAME TO LOVE—AND STILL DO—ABOUT HABITAT IS THE TEAMWORK INVOLVED.

"Deshaun, what's going on?" Mom demanded.

"Just wait," I answered as I kept tugging her inside. We finally reached the room, and with one last pull, I drew her into the space.

This, I announced, was mine. After years of sharing rooms with my siblings, I finally had a spot that was just for me.

Eventually, in 2006, our house was done, and we were ready to move in. Our new suburban home seemed thousands of miles away from the place we were leaving. It was clean. There was no paint peeling off the walls.

Perhaps even more important, the surrounding neighborhood was quiet. There were no sounds of gunfire or fistfights or family arguments spilling out into the street. It was so quiet that it took us a while to get used to it.

We knew we wouldn't be able to buy everything we would want to make our new home look nice, but in Mom's typical style, she told us not to worry about that. We would just focus on what we had, which was a brand-new house that was clean and safe. And we had helped build it. Even for an eleven-year-old boy, it was an amazing experience. I couldn't wait to tell visitors that I had hammered that nail over here or helped carry the beam over there. The night before we moved in, I was so excited that I almost couldn't sleep.

But it got even better. As we pulled into the driveway for the first time, I drew my breath in surprise. There was Warrick Dunn, star running back for the Atlanta Falcons. Dunn's charity, Homes for the Holidays, had been working in partnership with Habitat by supplying furniture, computers, housewares, and food to dozens of families since its founding in 1997. Now it was our turn. Dunn's organization had furnished our home from top to bottom. Dunn handed the keys to my mom and posed for photos. I could barely stand still, what with a new home and a football star welcoming us!

My palm was sweaty as I shook Dunn's hand. Shy as always, I managed to introduce myself and thank him. Mom fought back tears—she didn't want to be seen crying in photos capturing the moment.

It was the start of a better life for our family. We were in a safe area of town. I had my own bedroom, furnished by a guy I idolized! As I grew and continued to mature, Dunn's example never left me. I had seen the generosity, bordering on joyous obligation, that drove him, and I understood that people who have been truly blessed are privileged to share with others who are far less fortunate.

It didn't really occur to me at the time, but thinking about it later, I recognized the leadership and selflessness my mom displayed throughout the entire process leading up to our new home. Through my mother's force of will, she had overcome almost unimaginable obstacles.

> PEOPLE WHO HAVE BEEN TRULY BLESSED ARE PRIVILEGED TO SHARE WITH OTHERS WHO ARE FAR LESS FORTUNATE.

Unlike so many others, we were able to escape the recycling bin that was the government housing project. Mom's determination allowed us to become exceptions to the rule.

Not long after, we received a gift from my teacher, Mrs. Frierson, the one who had encouraged me to do the best I could in sports as well as in the classroom. She wanted to give me a Christmas present, in part to celebrate our new home. So she and her husband brought over a basketball goal. I had played on many basketball courts, but I had never had a goal of my own—until now.

It was freezing that day, so we all waited inside watching TV while Mrs. Frierson's husband and brother-in-law assembled the goal in our driveway. I lost count of how many Food Network shows we watched (not the most exciting of viewing choices for a young boy, but that was the decision of the group). They had thought it would be a fast job, and they finally finished some two hours later. By then it was dark. But they didn't stop working until it was finished. They kept at it because Mrs. Frierson's husband wanted to make sure I got to make the first basket.

When I made that shot, I didn't need to pretend to be someone else. I could be me.

Happily, many years later while I was at Clemson, I was thrilled to return the Friersons' generosity. I was home on spring break my freshman year, and Mrs. Frierson's nephew, Max, was turning four years old. His parents were throwing him a Deshaun Watson–themed party. I surprised him by showing up at the party. We ate cake, played games, and went to a children's museum—it was awesome. When it comes to serving someone as inspiring and generous as Mrs. Frierson, who is now a school principal, I wouldn't have it any other way.

Sometimes people think they don't have enough to share with others, but I don't think we always need to focus on giving other people things. You may not have money to share, but maybe you have time. Focus on that, and find a way to help someone who doesn't have that precious resource. That's why I love Habitat for Humanity so much. Most of those volunteers contribute through work and sweat, not a checkbook.

YOU MAY NOT HAVE MONEY TO SHARE, BUT MAYBE YOU HAVE TIME.

So many people pitched in to help our family out in those years, and I wouldn't be who I am without their generosity. It wasn't just *things* that they shared; they gave their time, which was in many ways more valuable. My mom may not have had the money to buy a house to get us out of the projects, but she was willing to put in her time to help at Habitat for Humanity, and in doing so, she improved not only our lives but the lives of others as well.

As it turned out, our family would soon need to rely on the help of others more than we expected.

In 2011, near the start of my sophomore year in high school, my mom was battling a sore throat that persisted for weeks. Suspecting she had strep throat, she finally went to the doctor. They decided to run a series of tests.

When the results came back, the doctor told her she didn't have strep.

I remember the day my mom called me into the family living room after I got home from football practice. She'd been crying. She told me that her never-ending sore throat was actually tongue cancer—stage 5. She had tried to keep it a secret from us as long as possible but realized that she had to tell us all the truth.

I started bawling. I didn't know what else to do or how to react. I thought having cancer meant she was going to die for sure. That was my mindset: people who got cancer died. Simple as that.

Aggressive treatment began right away. My mom spent about eight months at Emory University Hospital in Atlanta. She endured surgery to remove a section of her tongue, followed by a reconstructive procedure, then chemotherapy and radiation. She lost her hair. She couldn't even speak.

Mom didn't want us kids to visit her. Not only did she not want us to see what she looked like, but she didn't want to burden us any further than we already were. She was gone for my entire sophomore year. I saw her maybe two or three times during her eight months of treatment. I guess she figured that the whole situation would somehow be less upsetting if we didn't see what was happening to her.

Still, I called Mom on the phone nightly. I would talk to her, and then I would wait for her to write down what she wanted to say, and a nurse would read it to me.

Spoiler alert: My mom recovered and, as of this book, is cancer-free. She even managed to learn how to speak all over again after her treatment. But the whole experience emphasized the importance of focusing on what we had, even while my siblings and I were so acutely aware of what we didn't have: our mom's presence.

For one thing, we had the support and strength of family and friends. While my mom was away, my aunt Sonia and uncle Terri would sometimes host me and my three siblings—my older brother Detrick, then twenty-one, and twins Tyreke and Tinisha, age twelve. Other nights I'd stay with my best friend, Fred Payne. Another aunt, Yolanda Glasper, also was of enormous help during this time.

In addition, we had a supportive community. When my mom was diagnosed with cancer, we had almost no money. The town tradition in Gainesville was for all the high school students to have breakfast together at the Longstreet Cafe every Friday morning. Even though I couldn't pay for it, owner Tim Bunch let me dine free of charge so I could eat with my fellow students. He didn't see it as charity. In his eyes, we were a tight community. When someone in that community needed a helping hand, you didn't slap labels on it. You did something to help.

Others stepped up too. Hearing we were short on money, the local tax assessor's office gave me my first job. Superior Court Judge Andy Fuller gave me a second job organizing court case files. He even went so far as to give me a key to the courthouse so I could work after football practice. I eventually took on another job as a real estate assistant. Money was a priority, and I was determined to make as much as possible. With my mom away receiving cancer treatment, we needed every penny.

WHEN SOMEONE IN THAT COMMUNITY NEEDED A HELPING HAND, YOU DIDN'T SLAP LABELS ON IT. YOU DID SOMETHING TO HELP.

My routine was set. I'd get up in the morning, go to school, attend football practice, go to work after hours at the courthouse until about ten o'clock, go home, and somehow manage to fit in my homework along the way. That was the case Monday through Wednesday. I'd rest on Thursday, play a game on Friday night, and take Saturday off. On Sunday I'd head to church and then back to work that afternoon. Then I'd start the whole cycle over again the next week.

It was exhausting. But I kept focusing on the things we did have, which included a strong family. I wanted to do everything I could to keep our household as steady as it could be. In a way, I was trying to fill the role that my mom had handled for so many years without a single word of complaint.

My mom's battle with cancer gave me a valuable new perspective. There she was, a shell of her former self, fighting every day for her life but all the while focused on making sure her family was safe and taken care of. She wanted our lives to be as normal as possible under painful, anxious circumstances.

I had a great deal on my plate. I grew tired of school, the demands of football, and having to deal with an ill parent while my peers were free to just be high school kids. I was envious of the freedom they seemed to take for granted.

But then I would think about my mom and how hard she had worked for so many years to provide for our family and to give us a better life. While I was complaining about watching film or studying a playbook, she was off in Atlanta fighting the toughest battle of her life—all the while displaying a level of strength that I never thought anyone could have. When I started to feel sorry for myself, I'd remember her and what she was enduring. The pity party ended quickly every single time.

I came to see my mom in a completely different light. Sure, I'd always known how much she had sacrificed while we were growing up, but her illness gave me a genuine sense of the way she had led our family, both when she was well and when the cancer ripped through her body. She knew what she had to do as our matriarch because she knew just what we needed.

This brings me to another way I learned early on to focus on what I had instead of what I didn't have. As I already mentioned, I've only seen my father a few times. Even though I tried not to let it get to me, it was painful not having a father around. All my friends had fathers. At times it seemed unfair and even cruel to be the exception to the rule. Again, I was envious of others who had someone in their lives that I did not. Even those friends whose parents were divorced or separated had both a mother and a father—granted, two people who might not have been living together anymore, but still two parents. I felt cheated.

My mom's example helped me get past that mindset. Instead of wishing for something that simply wasn't going to happen, I looked to my mom as the adult I was going to rely on, the person I'd always focus on. She was there, doing everything she could for our family, and my father was somewhere else. I had to bend and adapt to that reality instead of wishing things were different because they never were going to be.

I was blessed with father figures who stepped up and lent their advice, strength, and encouragement—people like Coach Michael Perry and Jack Waldrip, whom you'll read about in the next chapter. If my dad had been around, I don't know that I would have developed relationships with these men, and I can't imagine not having them in my life. In some ways, I think I was actually better off not having my dad compared to some of my teammates whose fathers were present but caused pain in other ways. Instead, my mom stepped in to be basically my mother and father.

That, among other reasons, is why I refer to my mom as my rock. Her steadiness and strength have always stood out. She is the reason I try to be grateful for the things that are going right in my life instead of worrying about the things that aren't. Her optimism and strength inspire me to try to model her positivity, and I hope they will inspire you to do so as well.

PASS IT ON

- Consider the last time you took part in some sort of activity or service that benefited others. Think about how your participation helped improve other people's lives or advance a cause. What can you do in the future to replicate that experience? Can you position yourself to take part in something of even greater importance?
- It's so easy to get caught up worrying about the things you don't have. Take some time to make a list of all the things you do have and are grateful for. Take it a step further and reach out to the people who have supported you and shared with you to thank them.
- Take one day to pay specific attention to how you put others first. At the end of the day, write down how many examples you can recall. The next day, see if you can add to the list. Keep going, and record your growth in your willingness to put others ahead of yourself.

YOUR CHALLENGE

Find an organization or charity that supports your ideals and beliefs, and reach out to see how you can become involved with what that group is doing. If you're in a place to give financially, give generously, but giving of your time is just as important and can have lasting rewards.

IF YOU WANT TO SUCCEED,
YOU HAVE TO KNOW WHAT
YOU WANT TO ACHIEVE
AND PUT IN THE WORK
AHEAD OF TIME TO GET THERE.

CHAPTER 3

PREPARE FOR SUCCESS

High school is always an important time in life, and although I wouldn't necessarily label my high school years as the most enjoyable, they were certainly memorable.

During those years I did a lot of learning in classrooms, on the football field, and at home, and that learning helped me understand that success is all about preparation. If you want to succeed, you have to know what you want to achieve and put in the work ahead of time to get there. I started to grasp this lesson even before I had my first day as a high school student.

I spent the summer before my freshman year of high school working as a ball boy at the Atlanta Falcons' practice facility, which was just ten minutes away from my home. I got the job through the Boys & Girls Club in Gainesville. At my mom's encouragement, I'd begun attending the Boys & Girls Club when I was seven. In addition to sports, I really enjoyed the Passport to Manhood program that allowed me and my friends to discuss our goals and challenges in an open and frank manner.

That summer I was one of a few high school students chosen to take part in the ball boy program, which was started by Falcons owner Arthur Blank. As a ball boy, I picked up footballs during practice, took care of the team's equipment, and folded towels. Anything that the players needed, we ball boys took care of.

It was an incredible experience, and being a ball boy helped me see up close what was possible for my future if I remained determined and focused on my goals.

> BEING A BALL BOY HELPED ME SEE UP CLOSE WHAT WAS POSSIBLE FOR MY FUTURE IF I REMAINED DETERMINED AND FOCUSED ON MY GOALS.

It didn't hurt that the job had some surprising financial benefits. One time cornerback Asante Samuel forgot his mouthpiece in the locker room and asked me to get it for him. When I walked by his locker after practice, he pulled out this Louis Vuitton bag and gave me a $1,000 tip—just for getting his mouthpiece. He didn't have to give me anything, but he did. It was a real lesson on how to treat others and the importance of generosity, but particularly on showing generosity to those who will genuinely appreciate the spirit behind it.

I got to see how the players worked together as a team and the unity and bonding that were important parts of that. I was also lucky enough to become close with several of the players. I played catch with wide receiver Julio Jones and quarterback Matt Ryan. Although it was an informal thing, I took the time to watch these two consummate pros while we played. I noted the various angles that Matt used when throwing the ball and the position of his arm. I studied Julio and how he watched every single ball come into his hands. Even in the most casual game of catch, he was working on a consistent, reliable style of catching.

On a more organized level, the team had me take part by throwing to some of the wide receivers as part of their drills. I hit most every receiver squarely between the numbers, but I would really tense up when throwing to the starters. My throws to them betrayed the nerves I felt.

That was more than enough reason for some of the players to start giving me a hard time. Wide receiver Roddy White kidded me about being the star young quarterback who had a habit of throwing balls into the ground.

"How you supposed to be that good and you throwing bad balls?" Roddy asked me.

"You guys make me nervous," I replied with complete honesty.

Roddy looked at me in surprise. "Nervous? We're at practice."

"It's different throwing to high school players and throwing to you guys," I answered. With that, Roddy smiled ever so slightly. He could see how a kid could be intimated by being around gifted professionals. He let up on his ribbing, but only just a little bit.

Even though the players gave me a hard time for tightening up, I did well enough that I was asked back by the Falcons each year I was in high school. But the players continued to get on to me, although in an obviously friendly way.

Sometimes the guys would rib me about how quiet I was. Roddy once asked me, "If you never talk, how are people supposed to know who you are?"

"I'm just out here on the grind," I replied immediately.

Even though I was just one of a number of ball boys, Roddy made me feel like part of the team. He encouraged a feeling of belonging, and I appreciated it.

This was a lesson in leadership. Roddy clearly understood the importance of inclusion, of making certain that everyone associated with the team felt like they were a part of something bigger. Great leaders are like that. They never want others to feel as though they don't belong. If that's the case, a leader works to address that.

My ball boy experience helped prepare me for what was to come by giving me a glimpse of what the life of an NFL player was like. I knew that I wanted to play in the NFL, and once I knew what I was striving for, I could take the steps needed to get there.

That's why I took every opportunity to pay close attention to the details and specifics of practice. I studied various players' routines—when they arrived for practice, what regimen they followed, how their level of focus could shift depending on what they were working on each day. I also began to notice how certain players approached practice differently than others. They'd show up early, and they continued working on certain skills long after others had headed out the door. Their level of commitment and preparation truly stood out.

MY BALL BOY EXPERIENCE HELPED PREPARE ME FOR WHAT WAS TO COME BY GIVING ME A GLIMPSE OF WHAT THE LIFE OF AN NFL PLAYER WAS LIKE.

Athletics continued to fill much of my time once I became a student at Gainesville High School. I made the football team as a quarterback—luckily for me, not just any quarterback. My work ethic, attitude, and performance (I completed twenty-two out of twenty-five passes during my very first scrimmage) so impressed head coach Bruce Miller that he chose me as the starter, beating out a junior with two years' experience. At just fourteen years old, I was only the third freshman quarterback Coach Miller had ever started. All that play on the streets and fields of Gainesville was starting to pay off. I was humbled, but being as young as I was, also a bit intimidated.

My role as starting quarterback allowed me to pursue what was fast becoming an outright love of learning. I studied and prepared for every game just as much as I studied and prepared for my classes. I have always been like this. Childhood friends still recall how I would map out plays when we were playing football. I'd grab a stick and outline passing routes—down here ten feet, then cut left, that sort of thing. Many of my friends would just shake their heads in bewilderment as they tried to follow my ideas. If nothing else, my love of preparation taught me an early lesson about the value of clear communication for everyone involved.

Fortunately, Coach Miller's confidence in me was justified. Our team had one of the best records in its history that year, with ten wins and just two losses. I also had a solid season, throwing for more than 2,000 yards with seventeen touchdown passes and rushing for an additional 569 yards. I also scored five touchdowns on the ground.

> MY ROLE AS STARTING QUARTERBACK ALLOWED ME TO PURSUE WHAT WAS FAST BECOMING AN OUTRIGHT LOVE OF LEARNING. I STUDIED AND PREPARED FOR EVERY GAME JUST AS MUCH AS I STUDIED AND PREPARED FOR MY CLASSES.

In fact, my season was so solid that several Division 1 college football programs began to express an interest in me.

During my freshman season, the upperclassmen on the team started calling me "Rookie." At first they were just trying to give me a hard time, but the nickname eventually stuck as their way of telling me that I belonged. I was one of them—a realization that made me work harder to live up to their confidence. Like Roddy White of the Atlanta Falcons, they knew how essential it was to foster a sense of team in which nobody was left out or made to feel less important.

My education continued off the field as well. One day during my freshman year, I found a twenty-dollar bill lying on the ground outside of the high school. Unsure what to do, I brought the money to Coach Miller. He stuffed the bill into his desk drawer. A few weeks later, as nobody else had claimed it, Coach said the money was mine. Even as I put the money in my pocket, I couldn't help but think of the person who had lost that twenty dollars. I was happy to have the extra cash but felt badly for the person whose loss was my gain. I knew I would never want to benefit at someone else's expense.

At the beginning of my sophomore year, I met a man who literally changed my life—Michael Perry, the team's recently hired quarterbacks coach.

Having watched me my freshman year, Coach Perry said he had all the confidence in the world about my talent. What I needed was a work ethic every bit as strong. He made me understand that talent without an accompanying work ethic is only half the formula for success—and one without the other can only compromise your efforts.

As I like to say, Coach Perry's secret was that he didn't have a secret, some magical, mystical methodology to take ability and mold it into all that it could be. He just made me work my butt off. Simple as that. And the payoff went far beyond winning on the football field.

Coach Perry was the first to help me see that success of any kind is the result of focus, effort, and, especially, exhaustive preparation. His ability to convey that message to me and other teenagers was particularly remarkable. If you're coaching eighteen- or nineteen-year-olds, the value of intensive study and preparation can easily fall on deaf ears. To Coach's credit, he was able to impress on us not only the value of preparation in terms of football but that those habits would benefit us for the rest of our lives. That's a big idea for teens to get their heads around, but Coach got it across to us.

> TALENT WITHOUT AN ACCOMPANYING WORK ETHIC IS ONLY HALF THE FORMULA FOR SUCCESS—AND ONE WITHOUT THE OTHER CAN ONLY COMPROMISE YOUR EFFORTS.

To that end, Coach Perry started by giving me an enormous notebook of plays and defensive schemes. He instructed me to commit every detail to memory. I spent hours studying that book, making sure I absorbed everything it could teach me.

Then there was film work. That's an element of preparation I've come to realize is as important as any in a player's development. For those of you who have never done it, film work is essentially sitting in front of a screen and watching a video of a game, reviewing every play, often in slow motion, over and over. You look for what you did right and what you can improve on. You also watch other players, studying the workings of teams you're going to be up against and trying to figure out what plays they might try to use against you.

For me, film work is beneficial on so many levels. You can review a particular play over and over until you learn as much as you can. On the football field, things happen way too fast for that kind of study or reflection to be possible.

I believe film study is what separates the good players from the great ones. That's because, to be honest, film work can be pure drudgery. It's boring and repetitive. For athletes used to having their bodies in motion, sitting and staring at a screen for hours on end is borderline torture. Although technologies such as laptops and tablets make the process go faster, for lots of players, film study is a chore, pure and simple. They'd rather be playing, not watching.

I take a different approach. For me, film study represents an enormous opportunity to improve, to take what time I need to break down the specifics of my play and that of others. It appeals to the student in me; film work makes you that much more prepared when the time comes to perform.

> I BELIEVE FILM STUDY IS WHAT SEPARATES THE GOOD PLAYERS FROM THE GREAT ONES.

It also gets back to a point I raised earlier about the importance of balancing athletics with classroom work. As I mentioned, athletes who aren't students often fail to reach their full potential as players and people. Film study lets an athlete leverage the student inside to improve physical and mental performance.

Although every player approaches film study differently, I've always tried to cover certain factors, including:

Reading coverage: I look to see what sort of defense cover schemes other teams are running so I know what routes my receivers should be running and where I should be throwing the ball.

Understanding defensive fronts: How the opposing defense lines up determines blocking responsibilities.

Identifying blitzes: I look for signs and tendencies of a blitz where the defense commits additional players to rushing the quarterback. Receivers may run "hot" or short routes if a blitz occurs; alternatively, running backs may have to stay in the backfield to strengthen pass protection.

Pinpointing and correcting mistakes: Film lets you watch when you mess up and discover what you can do to make sure it doesn't happen again.

How many hours have I spent looking at film? Frankly, I've lost count. The more film time I put in, the better prepared I am. I don't think there's even such a thing as too much film time. When it comes to time spent in the film room, I stopped looking at my watch long ago. Its value goes way beyond minutes and seconds spent.

Studying film has helped me improve my own play, and it has given me the opportunity to study my teammates' play as well. That allows me the chance to offer feedback and suggestions so our entire team can improve.

My time with Coach Perry was grueling at first. I would arrive at school at 7:00 a.m. Coach Perry and I would have sausage biscuit sandwiches for breakfast, courtesy of the nearby Longstreet Cafe, then turn on the projector for a solid two hours. Head coach Miller started calling me a "film hound," someone who goes hunting for new film, who can't get enough of it. I studied great college quarterbacks as well as NFL icons like Peyton Manning and Tom Brady. Watching them perform over and over, I broke down their ability to do what they did and tried my best to make it work for me as well.

This went on both during the school year and over summer break, for four or sometimes five days a week. That was our routine, and it never varied. When school was in session, I'd head off to a full day of classes after our film study. Later on I'd go to Coach Perry's home, where he would quiz me on everything from offensive strategies to audibles to defensive formations. Then it was back home to do my schoolwork and prepare for the next day.

When I met Coach Perry, I was a football player. He turned me into a quarterback, a real student of the game who not only executes on the field but is capable of being involved in play calling and overall strategy. He helped me become a more complete player, both physically and mentally.

Coach Perry was more than just a coach to me. He made sure I focused on my schoolwork, that athletics never got in the way of academic performance. He constantly asked me if I was getting my homework done and how my grades were. He wanted to know which subjects I enjoyed the most and which ones I found more challenging. Like others had, he strengthened the bond between my schoolwork and athletics.

> WHEN I MET COACH PERRY, I WAS A FOOTBALL PLAYER. HE TURNED ME INTO A QUARTERBACK.

He also helped me move closer to God. He taught me what it meant to be a true man, a person of character and humility. He taught me the value of putting others before yourself. He was a father figure to me, something I'd never had growing up.

———————

Happily, Coach Perry was not the only person I looked to as a father figure. It was about this time that I met Jack Waldrip. A local real estate broker, Jack was heavily involved in the local Boys & Girls Club.

The outreach coordinator at the club kept trying to convince Jack that two teenagers would benefit from meeting and getting to know him. Jack, a sixty-some-year-old white man who had just undergone bypass surgery, was doubtful he would connect with two young African American boys. Since we were football players, Jack assumed that we might communicate better with someone younger, someone perhaps a bit closer to the game. But the people at the Boys & Girls Club as well as Jack's wife, Violet, continued to urge him to give the introduction a try.

Finally, Jack said okay. And, fortunately for me, I was one of those two young boys.

One day my friend Fred Payne, a defensive player who was outgoing and always talking, and I pulled in to Jack's driveway.

Of course, Fred started talking with Jack almost immediately while I hung in the background, quiet and shy as always. Eventually, though, Jack introduced himself, shook my hand, and we began talking.

We bonded almost instantly.

Jack has been a major force in my life ever since. We've spent a lot of Christmases together. He gave me lifts to the airport. He helped me celebrate major victories in my life and consoled me during times of trial. Jack even went so far as to name his dog Watson. What greater honor could a young man ask for?

The support of both of these men helped prepare me mentally and emotionally for the road ahead. At the end of my freshman year of high school, the legendary Coach Dabo Swinney at Clemson University reached out to me. He said he had known of me for the better part of a year and had come to appreciate my talent as well as my coachability. He then offered me a full scholarship to Clemson. I knew that this meant getting a college education without having to go into debt or needing my mom to pay a dime toward my degree, not to mention a genuine shot at making it to the NFL.

Naturally, I had heard of Coach Swinney well before this. He had been at Clemson since 2003, trying to boost a program in the ultra-competitive Atlantic Coast Conference (ACC). In fact, that was one of the most intriguing parts of his interest in me—I wanted to join a team that was looking to rise amid grueling competition, not just some power-house comfortably atop a so-so conference. The challenge appealed to me, as did the man trying to make it all happen.

His was an amazing and flattering offer. It was many things: thrilling, humbling, and a bit overwhelming. But what really won me over to Clemson was a promise from Coach Swinney. If I agreed to attend Clemson, he said, he would not recruit a quarterback the following year. His plan was to build the program around me.

> I WANTED TO JOIN A TEAM THAT WAS LOOKING TO RISE AMID GRUELING COMPETITION, NOT JUST SOME POWERHOUSE COMFORTABLY ATOP A SO-SO CONFERENCE.

At first I was a bit skeptical. *Right*, I told myself, *I'm sure I'm going to hear the same line from every coach hoping to lure me to his school.* They were all full of great promises.

But another thing I was beginning to learn was to trust the vibe I was feeling from someone else. I was gaining confidence in recognizing the energy that others give off. You can't put your finger on it or necessarily describe it to others, but it's there. I was learning to trust my gut, as you should learn to trust your own. It's rarely wrong.

Coach Swinney had vibes to spare. When he said something while looking you squarely in the eye, you just knew that he meant what he said and that he would do everything possible to make it happen. What I heard didn't carry a shred of doubt or uncertainty.

Coach Swinney's position of leadership was crystal clear. As I came to appreciate later, he led with absolute clarity and honesty. If you did something well, he'd congratulate you. If you messed up, he'd critique you in an equally blunt manner. He never wanted even the least bit of confusion in anyone's mind about what he was saying and why he was saying it. That drew me to him.

So, after thinking about it and praying for guidance, I committed to Clemson—one of the best decisions I've ever made. I made another good decision shortly thereafter.

Since my classroom and football experiences underscored the importance of preparation, it occurred to me that now might be an ideal time to do a little planning and preparation for what I wanted to achieve over the next several years.

> AFTER THINKING ABOUT IT AND PRAYING FOR GUIDANCE, I COMMITTED TO CLEMSON—ONE OF THE BEST DECISIONS I'VE EVER MADE.

I took out a piece of notebook paper and began to write. Thinking as I went along, I considered what sorts of major goals I wanted to achieve now that one of the first, biggest steps—committing to a major college football program—had been completed.

I wrote slowly:

- Win an ACC Championship
- Win a national championship
- Win the Heisman Trophy
- Graduate from Clemson within three years
- Move on to play in the NFL

That piece of paper is still in my childhood home. It means far too much to me to ever lose track of it. And seeing my goals spelled out like that gave me a plan and set me up to work as hard as it took to achieve them.

But the decision to eventually attend Clemson in no way clouded my commitment to Gainesville High School. During my high school career, I set numerous Georgia state football records, including total yards (17,134), total touchdowns (218), career passing yards (13,077), and career passing touchdowns (155). I also rushed for 4,057 yards and sixty-three touchdowns.

More important, the team enjoyed great success. In addition to advancing to the state semifinals twice, we won the overall state title my junior year, beating Ware County 49–13 in the title game. I remember the bus ride home from the Georgia Dome. With highway patrol escorting the bus into Gainesville city limits, sirens filled the air. We arrived back at the high school well after midnight. Still, hundreds of fans were waiting to greet us and share in our joy and achievement. For me, the experience showed just how much our team meant to the community, how our success was theirs as well.

This came on the heels of the wild celebration that took place on the field after the game itself. As people charged from the stands onto the playing field, Coach Miller and the team's seniors gathered on a small stage to accept the championship trophy. At the time, I was standing next to Coach Miller's wife.

"Deshaun, you need to be up there," she told me, motioning toward the stage. "You're the reason we won this thing."

I shook my head and shrugged my shoulders. "It's not my turn," I replied.

At first she had a look of complete shock on her face. Then, bit by bit, she started to smile. She understood completely how I felt and what I was trying to say.

As a servant leader looking to continually grow, I realized I had more to achieve. However wonderful it was to win the state championship, this was just one of my goals. Plus, I was not yet a senior, and the stage was occupied only by seniors. I knew my time would come. This was theirs.

The next fall I graduated from high school early. I wanted to be on Clemson's campus as soon as I could to take part in spring workouts, since I knew that the more practice time I had with this new team, the more ready I would be when it came time to play my first game.

AS A SERVANT LEADER LOOKING TO CONTINUALLY GROW, I REALIZED I HAD MORE TO ACHIEVE.

I firmly believe that preparation is one of the most important tools for success. Preparation makes me better positioned to succeed on the field, and it also occupies my mind as I get ready for a game. It's a way for me to chill, and, once I'm on the field, preparation allows my instincts to kick in and take over.

In that sense, preparation allows me to relax. Then, once it's time to perform, I'm physically and mentally at my peak to excel.

PASS IT ON

- Consider the last time you had to prepare for something important—a test, a presentation, a speech, anything you can remember. How did you go about preparing for it? Was there any method to how you prepared? What was the outcome? Were you pleased or disappointed with the results?

- Have you ever made a list of your goals? Take the time to come up with a list of things you want to accomplish—that's the first step toward making them happen. I encourage you to consider short-term goals (one year or less) as well as five- and ten-year goals.

- For me, film study is as much about reviewing my own mistakes as it is learning about other players. Do you ever take the time to review your own performance and think about how you can improve? Ask for feedback from your peers, or find a way to review your wins and losses and think about how you can improve next time.

YOUR CHALLENGE

The next time you prepare for something important, pay as much attention to your preparation as to what you're preparing for. Think about the steps you need to take, and write them down. Then, when you think you're ready, take a bit more time to prepare even more. Record the results and determine if the extra bit of preparation made a difference.

I LEARNED THAT I WANTED TO BE THE KIND OF LEADER WHO DOESN'T BACK DOWN FROM A CHALLENGE, STAYS COMMITTED TO THE GOALS HE'S LAID OUT, AND ALWAYS KEEPS HIS WORD.

CHAPTER 4

YOUR WORD IS YOUR OATH

Because I committed to Clemson so far in advance of graduating from high school, my decision stirred up a bit of anxiety and, to be blunt, outright gossip.

Deshaun Watson says he's going to Clemson, but what is he doing spending a weekend at Auburn? How many other schools are trying to lure him away, tempting him to back off from his dedication? There must be some school out there that's making a better offer!

That sort of chatter continued even after I began my Clemson career and we captured a national championship. After we won the national title, I remember seeing a blog that repeatedly asked how I had ended up at Clemson. *Where were the Georgia Bulldogs when this kid was available? How about in-state rival South Carolina? Who else was asleep at the switch?*

It's all kind of funny now, but the experience showed me what dedication is all about in an environment of doubt and speculation. Here, dedication meant blocking out a lot of the static and noise, sticking to my promise, and focusing on what I had to do to best follow through on my decision.

DEDICATION MEANT BLOCKING OUT A LOT OF THE STATIC AND NOISE, STICKING TO MY PROMISE, AND FOCUSING ON WHAT I HAD TO DO TO BEST FOLLOW THROUGH ON MY DECISION.

In actuality, my dedication to Clemson never wavered in the least. For one thing, it's not as though I was choosing a school whose program was completely in the tank. Over its history, Clemson has had many ACC championships as well as successful bowl game appearances. Additionally, part of the appeal for me was Clemson's dedication to develop the program with me as its centerpiece—I would be lying if I said that didn't hold a lot of sway.

This situation would also give me tremendous opportunities to work on my leadership skills. Had I gone to a different program, I would have likely had to share leadership with more established players. While I would have been perfectly happy to do that, I recognized that Clemson would offer me a more complete leadership role. That was something I wanted to embrace.

But, as I mentioned in the previous chapter, in talking with Coach Dabo Swinney, I could also sense his level of dedication. I could see the commitment in his eyes, the way he looked at me when he outlined what he intended to do and just how he would make it happen. I trusted that he was going to follow through. That was the sort of servant leader I aspired to be—someone who always kept his word. It was one of the most valuable lessons of leadership I took away from my decision to commit to Clemson: the absolute importance of keeping your word.

One of the first people I met after arriving at the Clemson campus never played football. But our first meeting turned out to be the beginning of a relationship as valuable as any I've had on the field.

Maria Herbst was and, as I write this, still is an academic advisor at Clemson. With a PhD, she's earned the privilege of being referred to as Dr. Herbst, but I call her Mama Maria.

Just as Coach Perry at Gainesville High made me into far more of a quarterback than I had been, Mama Maria made me into more of a student than I had ever been—and at times that wasn't a particularly easy job.

Mama Maria was my tutor at Clemson from the moment I arrived on campus until three years later when I graduated. When we first met, I told her that I planned to graduate from Clemson a year early. I didn't want to be one of those NFL players who leaves school for the pros only to wait twenty years or more to go back and complete his degree—or, worse, one who never bothers to go back at all. I had promised my mom I would graduate, and I wasn't about to pursue that goal halfheartedly.

My mom had impressed on me the value of an education. She insisted that it would give me options, and, unlike many other things in life, it was permanent.

> MY MOM HAD IMPRESSED ON ME THE VALUE OF AN EDUCATION. SHE INSISTED THAT IT WOULD GIVE ME OPTIONS, AND, UNLIKE MANY OTHER THINGS IN LIFE, IT WAS PERMANENT.

"Deshaun," she said, "you can never take away someone's education. As great a football player as you are, that's going to end eventually. But once you have an education, that's a part of you for the rest of your life. Never forget that."

Believe me, I never have.

I also wanted to challenge myself. It would have been less stressful to stay in school for the usual four years, but I wanted a difficult goal in front of me. I wanted to complete my education and move to the next step in my life as quickly and successfully as possible.

When Mama Maria heard of my plans to graduate in less than four years, she chuckled to herself. She was seated behind her desk in a small office space in Vickery Hall that was made bigger by Mama Maria's attention to organization. Obviously, she thought I was making some sort of joke. But seeing that I was dead serious, she quickly began offering advice.

"You're going to have to put in a heck of a lot of work to do that," she said in the forceful tone she would use when making an important point. As if I needed to be reminded, she told me that playing a significant role on a Division 1 football team was time-consuming enough, let alone trying to earn my diploma at a faster-than-usual pace. "Many people who don't play football can't find the time and commitment to graduate in three years," she added.

I was beginning to get a feel for what Mama Maria was all about. Above all, like Coach Swinney, she was straightforward. She wasn't going to sugarcoat anything about the challenge ahead of me. But she wasn't trying to discourage me. She was just being realistic and making sure that I knew full well what I would be up against. Once she realized that I was serious, she was completely on board. You could see it in the firm look of her eyes and the slight curl of a grin at the corner of her mouth. She was poised and ready to help in any way possible.

Once she knew I was committed, she was too.

So, I promised Mama Maria that I would, in fact, graduate in just three years, like I'd promised my mom. She agreed, and then we shook on it, my enormous hand cupping her significantly smaller one.

She didn't waste any time getting down to business. "Okay," she declared as we shook hands, "but I'm going to be on your rear like I'm your mama. Every single day. There will be no letup and no excuses. You can complain, but keep it to a minimum. We don't have time to waste on bellyaching."

I knew that Mama Maria meant every word. It was an important lesson for me. When you're taking on a challenge, especially a difficult one, it's critical to make certain everyone involved knows what will be expected of them. This was going to be far from a stroll in the park, and Mama Maria wanted to be sure I genuinely understood that.

As she had promised, Mama Maria stayed on my rear for the three years I spent at Clemson. She quickly learned how to connect with me. She saw how motivated and dedicated I was at heart; when I was tempted to take the easy way out—and there were times when I was sorely tempted to do just that—she knew exactly what to say. For instance, she knew how to push my competitive buttons when my commitment faltered.

I'd say something like, "I'm not gonna do this. It's good enough. I'm gonna take the L (loss) on that one."

Mama Maria would lock eyes with me. "Yeah," she'd say with a slight grin on her face, "I don't believe you're ever gonna take an L."

"Yeah, I guess I'll do it."

> WHEN YOU'RE TAKING ON A CHALLENGE, ESPECIALLY A DIFFICULT ONE, IT'S CRITICAL TO MAKE CERTAIN EVERYONE INVOLVED KNOWS WHAT WILL BE EXPECTED OF THEM.

She even got on me when I was away from school to accept an award. "At some point you just have to say no," she said in a teasing, scolding voice. "Don't you have enough awards already?" That made me laugh, but Mama Maria was making a point. As wonderful as awards and honors are, they shouldn't interfere with the task at hand. Commitment meant focusing on what was of genuine importance.

———————

As the school year got underway, I quickly learned where things were on the Clemson campus: my classes, dining halls, libraries, most every place I would need to be for the next several years. I still recall the first time I walked onto the field at Memorial Stadium, also known as "Death Valley." (Visiting teams gave the stadium that nickname, but it was also built close to a cemetery.) The stands seemed to rise all the way to the sky. Memorial Stadium has a capacity of more than eighty thousand—about double the population of the town I grew up in. I'll admit, it was daunting, particularly given my role as the would-be leader of the team those thousands of fans cheered for. Those first moments brought the challenge I was facing into perspective.

My football career at Clemson began from a viewpoint that I was frankly unaccustomed to: the sidelines. However intent Coach Swinney was on building the team around me, he still had a solid starting quarterback in senior Cole Stoudt. With Stoudt leading the team, I was determined to make the most of my backup role by learning as much as I possibly could. I studied, watched those

MY FOOTBALL CAREER AT CLEMSON BEGAN FROM A VIEWPOINT THAT I WAS FRANKLY UNACCUSTOMED TO: THE SIDELINES.

around me, and practiced with the focus and intensity of a starter. Remember: prepare, then prepare some more.

Even though I was second string, I still got a bit of playing time. Through three games, I completed twenty-nine of forty-one passes for 479 yards with four touchdowns and no interceptions. Meanwhile, Cole was struggling some as quarterback. He threw only eleven interceptions his entire college career, but ten of those were during his senior year. Cole's difficulties and my performance in limited duty eventually gave the coaching staff sufficient confidence to name me the starter.

I came out of the gate ready to perform. In my first career start against the North Carolina Tar Heels, I set a school record with six touchdown passes, throwing for 435 yards in a 50–35 Clemson victory.

But my freshman season was riddled with challenges—challenges that came in the heartless form of injuries. In October 2014, I broke a bone in my right hand while playing against the Louisville Cardinals. I left in the first quarter and never reentered the game. I missed the next three games as the bone took time to heal.

> MY FRESHMAN SEASON WAS RIDDLED WITH CHALLENGES— CHALLENGES THAT CAME IN THE HEARTLESS FORM OF INJURIES.

In our next game against Georgia Tech, I came out of the game with what I first thought was just a strain. I wasn't so lucky. I had torn my anterior cruciate ligament (ACL) in my left knee.

I sat out the next game against Georgia State. Most everyone expected I would have to miss the next game against in-state rival South Carolina, but I wasn't about to let that happen. Fitted with a brace, I continued to practice. The medical team gave me the go-ahead to play against Carolina, but with strict rules. No crazy scrambles. Get rid of the ball quickly. Go down before being tackled.

That all made sense, but I also knew the promise I had made to Coach Swinney that, as long as I was the quarterback, we wouldn't lose to Carolina.

And we won the game.

It was a very painful but powerful lesson in being willing to sacrifice yourself to keep your commitments.

I underwent surgery to repair my ACL the Friday before our postseason bowl game against Oklahoma. As my freshman year ended, I was all the more determined to make the next season memorable by preparing—then preparing even more.

Academics at Clemson were every bit as challenging as football. I took as many as twenty credit hours every semester to reach my goal. That included the summer as well as the conventional academic year. This was particularly tough; summer football workouts were longer and more physically demanding (South Carolina heat) and the academics were every bit as challenging, with classroom material getting compressed into a much shorter time frame than a usual semester. The term *summer vacation* didn't apply to me during my years at Clemson.

The regular season was no less demanding. One time I had three major tests the same week we were playing against rival Florida State University in one of the biggest games of that year. It was crazy trying to prepare for everything at once. I may have gotten some sleep, but I can't say for certain just how much. Still, I passed all three tests, and we won the game against FSU.

Even though that was a particularly tough stretch, my everyday regular-season schedule was anything but easy. My day often began at four o'clock in the morning, since that was the only way I could grab a shower and some breakfast prior to a 5:30 a.m. workout. Then I had classes beginning at nine for a full day, followed by 7-on-7 film study. Practice came after that. I fit in meals when I could.

I usually got back to my dorm room late in the evening. As I took a quick break before getting to my homework, I would enviously watch my roommate getting ready and heading out for an evening of fun with other people from the dorm.

Every so often the urge to grab my coat and go with him was almost overwhelming. I desperately wanted to hang with my boys, to be a regular college kid. I hungered for the kind of fun that so many others took for granted.

But keeping my promise to my mom, Mama Maria, and myself was far more important to me than any sort of evening entertainment. So, I'd turn on my desk-top lamp, sit down, and bury myself in my studies. I won't say it was easy, but I stuck with it, often still at the books when my roommate returned after a night out.

I DESPERATELY WANTED TO HANG WITH MY BOYS, TO BE A REGULAR COLLEGE KID. I HUNGERED FOR THE KIND OF FUN THAT SO MANY OTHERS TOOK FOR GRANTED.

Fortunately, I also had Mama Maria to keep me on track. She did more than her share to shore up my discipline when I started to waver. And she did not put up with any sort of excuses or pleas for a break. We were supposed to meet every day promptly at one in the afternoon, and more than once I called her intending to bail on our session.

"Mama," I'd say, trying to make myself sound exhausted to evoke even a shred of pity, "I just can't make it in today. Too much going on."

Inevitably, there would be a snort of disgust at the other end of the line. "Uh-uh. You'd better get your butt in here. We've got work to do!"

I always did as she told me.

Throughout my three years at Clemson, no matter what was happening on the football field, Mama Maria never let my focus on my schoolwork fade for even an instant. She knew what I wanted to achieve, and she was going to do her part to help me get there. She helped organize my notes and gave me study tips and advice on how to make the best use of my time when taking a test. Hers was an unquestioning support, and I recognized that.

She helped me prepare so thoroughly for my studies at Clemson that I took up the habit of texting her every time I finished a project, paper, or some other task. On several occasions late in the summer of my third year at Clemson, I texted Mama Maria that I was "down to five"—a countdown of how many credits I needed to graduate.

At Clemson, I began to understand that commitment meant sacrifice. It would always mean giving up something you wanted or valued to pursue a goal of far greater significance. As I watched my friends in school go to parties, play video games for hours on end, and just hang out, I couldn't join them. I had goals that I had promised myself and others I would achieve. If I wanted to keep my word to my mom and Mama Maria, I was going to have to give some things up. I was learning about the value of priorities.

Of course, it helped that the school's overall dedication to me went beyond my ability to play football. As I like to say, Coach Swinney helped me develop a hunger for education; Mama Maria made certain I remained hungry and committed to being the best student I could possibly be. Coach Swinney, Mama Maria, and Clemson all recognized that my athletic and academic goals would be challenging to achieve. None of them flinched in the face of those challenges. In that sense, dedication mandates challenging yourself—looking for obstacles to overcome instead of avoiding them. It's bonding with others as well as ideals, not based just on what may have occurred in the past but, through dedication, what you wish to bring to the future.

> AT CLEMSON, I BEGAN TO UNDERSTAND THAT COMMITMENT MEANT SACRIFICE. IT WOULD ALWAYS MEAN GIVING UP SOMETHING YOU WANTED OR VALUED TO PURSUE A GOAL OF FAR GREATER SIGNIFICANCE.

Dedication means not taking the easy way out, whether that's selecting a school based on more than just wins and losses or working with a student who's in a high-level athletic program but planning on graduating in only three years.

I learned that I wanted to be the kind of leader who doesn't back down from a challenge, stays committed to the goals he's laid out, and always keeps his word. With Coach Swinney, Mama Maria, and the entire Clemson community, I had wonderful and inspiring examples to follow.

PASS IT ON

- When you think of the importance of keeping your word, what does that mean to you? Does it mean keeping your word without exception or occasionally compromising it? How do you see that commitment in others? Do you admire those whose word is their bond, their pledge of honor? By the same token, how do you treat others who are not as committed to keeping their word? Do you have a different relationship with them than with those whose word you can always trust?

• Have you ever broken a commitment you've made? How did that make you feel? Were there repercussions? What can you do to make sure you do better in the future?

YOUR CHALLENGE

Commit to something that, on the surface, you're not really all that excited about. Maybe it's a project at work or a family matter. Even though you're not completely enthusiastic, try to stick to your word and maintain your commitment as much as possible. Once it's done, think about how you feel—was it particularly rewarding to keep your word when it would have been easy to beg off? Was it more rewarding than keeping your word about something you truly believe in?

LOSING FORCES INTROSPECTION—
NOT ONLY ABOUT WHAT
CONTRIBUTED TO THE LOSS BUT
ABOUT WHAT YOU PERSONALLY
CAN CHANGE TO ACHIEVE
SUCCESS MOVING FORWARD.

CHAPTER 5

FAILURE: THE BEST TEACHER THERE IS

I have no doubt that failure is the best teacher there is. It's blunt, unforgiving, and pulls no punches. And, in my case, one particular example of failure happened on one of the biggest stages you can imagine.

In 2015, Clemson compiled an undefeated 12–0 regular season and a No. 1 ranking in the polls. In the ACC Championship Game against No. 10 North Carolina, I threw for 289 yards and three touchdowns and ran for two more. Most important, we won the game, claiming the ACC Championship for the first time since 2011. On an individual level, I was also named the ACC Championship Game MVP.

We moved on to the College Football Playoff, selected as the No. 1 seed. In our first game of the tournament, we beat Oklahoma 37–17 in the Orange Bowl. I threw for 187 yards and a touchdown and ran for 145 yards and another touchdown.

Next up was the ultimate challenge: the championship game

against powerhouse Alabama. Between my passing and rushing yards—478 in total—I set the record for most total yards in national championship game history. But even though I threw for 405 yards and four touchdowns, we lost the game 45–40.

Special teams were a challenge for us all night in that particular game. Perhaps the most obvious example was Kenyan Drake's 95-yard touchdown on a kickoff return. At the time, it pushed Alabama to a double-digit lead. Making matters worse were Alabama's onside kick that led to a touchdown as well as a missed field goal by us. We had needed a complete game from all parts of our team, and we simply didn't deliver.

Still, honors and awards for me followed the national championship. I finished third that year in the voting for the Heisman Trophy, the most prestigious award in college sports. I won the Davey O'Brien Award, presented annually to the best college quarterback. I was also named the 2015 ACC Player of the Year and ACC Offensive Player of the Year.

All the awards and accolades were great, but I was devastated by the loss in the championship game. In a way, losing out on a national championship was more wrenching than it would have been if we'd never even gotten close to that point. I was deeply conflicted. I was getting all this praise for how I had played—and I knew I had played well—but all the praise in the world rings hollow when it's overshadowed by defeat. I wrestled with a flood of emotions for days on end.

But the Alabama game taught

> I WAS GETTING ALL THIS PRAISE FOR HOW I HAD PLAYED—AND I KNEW I HAD PLAYED WELL—BUT ALL THE PRAISE IN THE WORLD RINGS HOLLOW WHEN IT'S OVERSHADOWED BY DEFEAT.

me another lesson that's critical for being an effective servant leader. As I came to understand in the painful days following that devastating loss, losing is a far better teacher than winning. Granted, we all want to win, and winning makes you and those around you feel great. Everyone's happy when they're winning. You love everyone and everything.

But losing forces introspection—not only about what contributed to the loss but about what you personally can change to achieve success moving forward. And when you look inside yourself, that serves as a model for others to do the same. Losing is never fun, but, ultimately, everyone benefits if you approach it as an opportunity to learn and grow.

Looked at another way, losing makes you a student, whether you want to be one or not. If you don't study what went wrong, what you could have done differently, then it's obvious that you never cared much about the outcome in the first place. I've never met a single athlete who could just shrug off a loss without thinking about why it happened.

Losing, I've come to learn, also presents challenging leadership obstacles. For one thing, you first have to get over your own disappointment. Then it's up to you to help those around you do the same—to encourage them to learn everything they can from the experience while leaving much of the sting behind. Finally, as a leader, you have to point the way to rebound from failure.

Over the weeks that followed the Alabama loss, my teammates and I reviewed the game in exhausting detail. We looked at film of every play repeatedly, with attention to how each and every player on the field performed. We all wanted to see any sign, any hint of what might have gone wrong.

WHEN YOU COME UP
SHORT IN ANYTHING
YOU TRY TO ACHIEVE,
BE AS METICULOUS
AS YOU POSSIBLY
CAN BE IN STUDYING
HOW YOU FAILED TO
ACHIEVE SUCCESS.

That's a leadership lesson I've carried with me. When you come up short in anything you try to achieve, be as meticulous as you possibly can be in studying how you failed to achieve success. It can be humbling and even painful, but it's the best way to stop history from repeating itself.

That's how I knew what I needed to do going into my junior year.

My junior—and last—year as a student-athlete at Clemson was everything I had worked so hard to achieve. We had a great season, and after routing the powerhouse Ohio State Buckeyes 31–0 in the semifinal national playoff game, we once again faced off against Alabama. Since we had tangled with them before and come up short, we knew full well what we were up against. Many football analysts had said that, at their peak, the 2016 Alabama team's defense was one of the greatest in college football history. As quarterback and one of the on-field leaders on offense, I knew we all had to bring our very best effort.

While the game was tense and competitive throughout, things began to look bleak for us in the third quarter. The Crimson Tide were up by ten points—24–14. Under Coach Nick Saban's leadership, Alabama was known for finishing strong. If they were ahead by double digits at this point in the game, they were extremely likely to win. In other words, they didn't make a habit of losing as the clock ticked down. We knew that from the game a year prior when Alabama simply built too big a lead for us to overcome.

I had to step up.

The lead changed hands three times in the fourth quarter. It began when I found wide receiver Mike Williams open for a 4-yard touchdown barely a minute into the final fifteen to trim Alabama's lead to 24–21. Then, with a little more than four minutes left in the game, we seized our first lead when running back Wayne Gallman scored from a yard out.

Still, we knew Alabama was far from finished. The Crimson Tide moved down the field with a combination of efficiency and creative play calling. In a bit of razzle-dazzle, receiver ArDarius Stewart took a backward pass from quarterback Jalen Hurts and fired a strike to tight end O. J. Howard for 24 yards. Hurts broke loose the next play, escaping from a collapsing pocket and slipping past and through defenders for a 30-yard touchdown run to make the score 31–28 in favor of Alabama. Once again, the Alabama players showed that they rose to the occasion in crunch time.

There was 2:07 left on the clock.

You've probably heard about athletes and others who experience a remarkable level of calm and focus when everything around them is deafeningly loud and chaotic. The speed with which things occur seems to slow down dramatically. That's precisely how I felt when we got the ball back with the national championship on the line. In fact, I was so focused that I remembered what quarterback Vince Young said to his University of Texas teammates just before their last-second touchdown that defeated Southern California in the 2005 season championship game: "Let's be legendary."

That's what I said to my teammates as we huddled up. I felt this truth to my core. Three words that meant one thing: all the work, all the sacrifice, and all the dedication came down to just these few seconds. What happened was up to us—not just one person but everyone involved with the team.

I completed passes to Williams and tight end Jordan Leggett, both of whom made fantastic catches for large gains. But however much we had moved the ball, time was edging away. We were at first and goal with just fourteen seconds left.

We caught a break with a pass interference call on Alabama that placed the ball at the 2-yard line with six seconds remaining. In that moment, I thought that if we couldn't push the ball in, we were certainly close enough for a game-tying kick and overtime.

But my teammates and I were determined to be legendary. And, again, I really couldn't hear the crowd roaring in the background. I felt at peace and knew what I was going to do.

Being legendary didn't mean settling for a field goal.

> BEING LEGENDARY DIDN'T MEAN SETTLING FOR A FIELD GOAL.

Amid the tangle of bodies that collided after the ball was snapped, receiver Hunter Renfrow managed to slip past the defense. I took the snap, rolled right, and tossed the ball to Renfrow as lightly as though we were playing catch in the backyard.

It was one of the easier throws I'd made all night, but we were national champions as a result. For just the second time in Clemson football history, we stood at the top of the heap.

Overall, I ended up throwing for 420 yards and three touchdowns, good enough to be named the game's MVP. Every bit as satisfying was that, in two games against Alabama, I threw for a total of 825 yards and accounted for eight touchdowns. In the fourth quarter alone, I completed twelve of eighteen passes for 130 yards and two touchdowns.

From a team perspective, our twenty-one points were the most fourth-quarter points scored against the Crimson Tide the entire season.

―――――

It's difficult to express the emotions and experience of winning that national title. Naturally, our success was a culmination of grinding it out day in and day out, remaining focused, and, as I experienced in the title game itself, finding a sense of peace and balance when everything around us was noise and chaos.

It also showed the value of revisiting failure. By breaking down every aspect and element of the game we lost to Alabama the year before, our team was able to retool our game plan to take advantage of what we identified as Alabama's few vulnerable points. The painstaking effort had truly paid off.

I think we all learned another lesson from that first loss that helped us in the rematch. Simply put, the past is past. Move on when you've gotten everything you can out of an experience. Study it and go to school on it, but don't dwell on failure. If you're looking back all the time, it's impossible to see what you have in front of you. I know we as a team benefited from a forward-looking mindset. As for me, during those final seconds, the last thing I had on my mind was coming up short again.

On an individual level, I became the first player since 2004 to win the Davey O'Brien Award in consecutive seasons. I also won the Johnny Unitas Golden Arm

> SIMPLY PUT, THE PAST IS PAST. MOVE ON WHEN YOU'VE GOTTEN EVERYTHING YOU CAN OUT OF AN EXPERIENCE. STUDY IT AND GO TO SCHOOL ON IT, BUT DON'T DWELL ON FAILURE.

Award, given to a junior or senior college quarterback. While the award celebrates on-field performance, it also emphasizes character, scholastic achievement, and qualities of leadership. For me, that made the award much more than just a measure of athletic success.

But there were individual disappointments as well. Once again, I was one of the five finalists for the Heisman Trophy. Once again, I came up empty, with Louisville quarterback Lamar Jackson receiving the coveted award. I was disappointed but very happy for Lamar. He deserved it as much as anyone.

But, as I've stressed before, though personal achievements are fine and good, nothing comes close to the value of success as a team. A servant leader looks past individual success to consider the group as a whole. And, here, there were no disappointments.

I was learning to prioritize my leadership goals. While I didn't win certain individual awards, our team's national championship was of far greater importance to me. Failure was teaching me another valuable lesson: losing happens to everyone, but the sting doesn't hold on forever if you learn from the loss and get right back to work—becoming all the more prepared, both mentally and physically.

PASS IT ON

- How did you react the last time you failed at something that mattered a great deal to you? You were probably upset, but did you get caught up in your emotions? Did you do anything besides get angry and frustrated? Or did those emotions lead you to something constructive, something that you could do to better prepare yourself for success in the future?

- As a developing servant leader, consider how others impacted by that failure reacted to it. Was their reaction similar to yours? If so, did you do anything about that reaction or merely join in?

YOUR CHALLENGE

The next time you have to deal with a failure or setback, reevaluate your reaction. It's okay to be angry or frustrated, but instead of getting caught up in those emotions, make a conscious effort to focus on what you can gain from the experience that may prove useful moving forward. Review the events that led up to what occurred. Could you have changed anything that happened? Could you have prepared in a different manner? If it's helpful—and it probably will be—write down any ideas that occur to you. Bear your thoughts in mind the next time you encounter a similar situation or challenge.

MAINTAINING BALANCE
MEANS YOU ARE ABLE TO
KEEP YOUR HEAD
WHILE EVERYONE AROUND
YOU IS LOSING THEIRS.

CHAPTER 6

NEVER GET TOO HIGH, NEVER SINK TOO LOW

Winning the national title was the experience of a lifetime. But, to be honest, it didn't even come close to comparing with what took place a few weeks prior. That was when—outfitted in my cap and gown, wearing a multicolored bow tie—I walked across the stage at Littlejohn Coliseum in mid-December 2016 to receive my bachelor's degree in communications from Clemson.

I was the first person in my family to receive a college degree. My mom cried. Behind my smile that spread from ear to ear, I was crying a little bit myself. I could hear my siblings and other relatives cheering in the packed arena.

> I WAS THE FIRST PERSON IN MY FAMILY TO RECEIVE A COLLEGE DEGREE.

Shortly after the graduation, Clemson's Instagram account posted a picture of me receiving my degree. The post said:

"Walking across the stage as a proud Clemson graduate! Thank you Deshaun!"

No way, I thought the moment I saw it. I immediately posted my response:

"Noo, THANK YOU Clemson University! Best 3 years of my life!"

I meant that and still do.

As an aside, my determination to graduate in less than three years became fodder for others. I remember how Coach Swinney reacted one time as my graduation neared. I needed only five more credits to complete my degree, and during a press conference a reporter asked a question that sort of dissed what I was trying to achieve.

"How many of us here were five hours short of graduating in two-and-a-half years?" Coach Swinney shot back. "Raise your hand. Quick."

Silence.

"That's what I thought."

Even Mama Maria had some fun as my graduation neared. My last class, having to do with the importance of mental and emotional balance, seemed like just the sort of laid-back class that I wanted after so much hard work. Mama Maria purposely never told me that there would be a final paper I would have to write!

My time at Clemson taught me lessons I'll carry with me for the rest of my life. Not all of them took place on the football field. Those lessons and others were foremost in my mind when, on November 8, 2016, I announced I was declaring for the 2017 NFL Draft.

As the draft approached, football naturally dominated my thoughts. I had a great deal of excitement—and more than a little uncertainty.

On the one hand, being in a position to join an NFL team was the culmination of a lifelong dream. Now that I was on the edge of achieving it, I struggled to keep my emotions in check. I was hungry just to get started.

But, as I said, I was also anxious. Coming out of Clemson, most scouts and analysts projected I would be taken in the first round of the draft. *Sports Illustrated*, Pro Football Focus, and ESPN had all ranked me as the top quarterback available. NFLDraftScout.com had placed me second. Overall, the scouts placed me as high as the seventeenth overall prospect.

> BEING IN A POSITION TO JOIN AN NFL TEAM WAS THE CULMINATION OF A LIFELONG DREAM.

All that praise was wonderful to hear, but it still left many questions unanswered. Which team would select me? Just how high would I go in the draft? What if one or more other quarterbacks were selected before me? What would that say about how NFL scouts, executives, coaches, and others judged my talent?

Of course, there were doubters as well. Some scouts cautioned that I was still inexperienced in reading defenses. Others questioned my decision-making. There was also some concern about my passing accuracy. (Since I could run as well as throw, some people assumed running would be my first choice rather than throwing the ball. Nothing could have been further from the truth.)

Two things in particular were helpful at this point. The first was the advice my friend Cam Newton had given me: *never get too high; never sink too low.* Cam, an NFL star quarterback, had sent me this advice in a text after our loss to Alabama my sophomore year, and it has stuck with me ever since.

I first met Cam at his 7-on-7 camp in Atlanta going into my junior year of high school. The camp was an intense exercise, using only seven players per side to focus on each individual's skills and execution. After the camp, Cam selected me to be the quarterback for the all-star 7-on-7 team he was going to take to nationals in Florida. He traveled down there with us, and I got the chance to talk to him and make a personal connection.

Understandably, I was in awe of Cam when I first met him. He was several years older than I was, and he was everything I aspired to be—a talented player with just enough swag to radiate confidence and not slide into cockiness. We clicked instantly.

Over the years he stayed in touch, texting or calling me every now and then just to see how I was doing or to ask if I needed anything. He became my mentor. Whenever I hear the nickname D-Watt—what Cam calls me—I know I'm going to learn something of value.

It was his text in the wake of the Alabama loss that really got me back on track emotionally.

Basically, Cam told me to stay as mentally balanced as possible—never letting the highs push you into the stratosphere or letting the lows drop you so much that you thought you'd never be able to get up again. Balance, he said, was everything. Taking success too much to heart left you vulnerable to disbelief when things went wrong. By the same token, immersing yourself in failure could make it seem more permanent than it was.

He also urged me to accept both love and hate—because when you're successful, you'll always have those who love you, but you'll also always have haters, people who will try to tear you down simply because it's what they do.

According to Cam, the sweetest way to make them shut their mouths is to win.

I took that advice to heart. It would have been all too easy to coast into my junior year of college having given up on both a national championship and my goal of graduating early. Based on the success I had enjoyed, I could have decided that I had earned my stripes. Let someone else do the heavy lifting. Instead, I turned my attention to those things that had gotten me to where I was: football and academics. Far better to stay even-keeled and focused rather than rushing into some sort of foolish knee-jerk reaction I would likely regret. So here I was, college degree in hand, looking toward the draft.

The second thing that made me feel hopeful was a pre-draft visit I had with the Houston Texans in April. During the visit, they interviewed me and then ran me through a series of questions to gauge my knowledge of strategy and general football IQ.

> FAR BETTER TO STAY EVEN-KEELED AND FOCUSED RATHER THAN RUSHING INTO SOME SORT OF FOOLISH KNEE-JERK REACTION I WOULD LIKELY REGRET.

It was both fun and challenging. One of the exercises involved my learning a particular route; more specifically, the offensive staff drew up a route on the whiteboard, erased it, then left the room for fifteen minutes. When they returned, I was supposed to be able to teach them the route as though they were seeing it for the first time.

When they came back, I walked them through the play as though the quarterback were right-handed. Then I flipped the mechanics of the play and showed them how it would go with a left-handed quarterback.

They were astonished. I just smiled and told them I knew that play like the back of my hand. I didn't say that to be arrogant. I wanted to show them the kind of quick study I could be.

All that lasted for most of the morning, and then we broke for lunch.

We went into the facility's cafeteria to eat. After I got my food, I didn't see anybody I really knew all that well, so I just sat down in the corner of the room to eat my meal. Other players started to drift over to join me. At first they were fellow Clemson grads such as defensive tackle D. J. Reader and wide receiver DeAndre Hopkins. Defensive end Jadeveon Clowney joined us not long after that—even though he had played for rival South Carolina, we decided to be generous and let him sit down.

Soon about twenty players were crowded into a tight circle. We pushed a couple of tables together so everyone could have a seat. I was flattered that even though the room was filled with a former No. 1 draft pick and many All-Pros, so many guys wanted to talk to me.

Immediately, I felt at home. Even though the draft hadn't happened yet, I felt I was in the right place. I thought I could really contribute to something special. The chemistry and vibe were there.

I also sensed a real opportunity for leadership. The Texans had done well the prior year, finishing first in the AFC South but losing in the divisional playoffs. Even though I would be a rookie—a complete newcomer to the team—I felt as though I could really help this team succeed with my play as well as my leadership.

By the time the draft approached, I was confident I had done pretty much all that I could to place myself in the best possible light, both professionally and personally. In many ways, there was nothing more

I could do. That helped me let go of a good deal of my nervousness. My agent, David Mulugheta, urged me to relax and enjoy the experience as much as possible. At this point, whatever happened, happened, he told me.

I think I've cried in public only once. That was on draft night, after the Houston Texans traded up in the draft field to select me twelfth overall. I was the third quarterback taken in the draft, after Mitchell Trubisky (Chicago Bears) and future star and Super Bowl champion Patrick Mahomes (Kansas City Chiefs). After all that hard work, my dream had finally come true.

> BY THE TIME THE DRAFT APPROACHED, I WAS CONFIDENT I HAD DONE PRETTY MUCH ALL THAT I COULD TO PLACE MYSELF IN THE BEST POSSIBLE LIGHT, BOTH PROFESSIONALLY AND PERSONALLY.

But my tears that night were about more than the reality that I had just been drafted into the NFL. They happened when I was on camera doing a post-draft interview. A member of the crew handed me a letter and asked if I was okay reading it out loud.

I opened it and saw that it was from my mother.

"Deshaun, when you came into this world, you brought a love to my heart that I had never appreciated," I read as my hands started to shake. "I watched you play your first flag football game, all the way to the last college game. To be here at the NFL Draft and see you walk across the stage is a dream come true. I'm so proud of you. I'm so proud of the person and the man you became. Making it to the NFL is an accomplishment that you made come true.

"That being said, it brings so much joy to my heart. I wish you love, happiness, and longtime success.

"As I look back, we was not supposed to be here."

When I read that, I had to stop. I bent over, my hands covering my eyes as I shook with tears. I tried to start reading again but struggled to regain some form of composure. Eventually, I was able to raise my head and finish reading Mom's letter to me.

"In the words of Drake: 'We made it.' Love, Mama."

As I finally managed to finish the letter, I looked up into the camera. A member of the TV crew asked me if there was anything I wanted to say in reply.

"Love you, Mama," I said, trying to grin through my tears. "We made it."

I took it further than that. To show my mom all that she means to me and how grateful I am for everything she's done for me and the rest of my family, I celebrated the draft results by buying her a brand-new car—a 2017 Jaguar.

I tried not to let myself get too high, but it sure was hard.

One month later I signed a four-year contract with the Houston Texans. It was time to get to work.

Going into training camp—held in West Virginia so we could escape the Texas heat in the heart of summer—I knew full well that I was not the No. 1 quarterback on the Texans' depth chart. That title belonged to Tom Savage, who had worked his tail off to win the starting job. I was eager to learn all that I could from Tom.

The first few days of workouts reinforced what so many people had told me. The NFL game is completely different—not just more involved and complicated but much faster paced as well. You had to learn fast and execute even faster. It became clear to me that quick decision-making was an absolute must. Players who made smart choices fast were the rule, not the exception. Everyone who played in this league was there for a reason.

I approached my first few days of professional football as an eager student. I watched others and drove myself to learn as much as I could about the Texans' system, studying hours of film and staying late after practice.

THE NFL GAME IS COMPLETELY DIFFERENT— NOT JUST MORE INVOLVED AND COMPLICATED BUT MUCH FASTER PACED AS WELL.

It began to pay off on the very first day of camp. I managed to get through that entire day without a major mental error—an achievement of which I was exceedingly proud. I missed no handoffs and never threw to the wrong receiver. But I knew I was going to make mistakes moving forward—and I did. I just tried to learn from them and, even more important, not make the same mistake twice.

Apparently, people noticed. I was getting feedback saying how coaches and other players were impressed with how quickly I was learning the Texans' system. Every bit as complimentary was a tweet from *Houston Chronicle* sports columnist John McClain:

"I covered Warren Moon from from Day 1 for 10 years. At his 3rd practice, Watson reminds me of Moon [in] his first camp in 1984. So smooth!"[1]

That was a very flattering thing for John to say about me, but my first professional training camp experience definitely involved a lot of work and learning on my part. John's words reminded me of the description of a duck on the water: on the surface, all seems fluid and effortless but, underneath, he's paddling like crazy. I tried not to read too much into it and not to get too high or too low.

One of the first things I came to appreciate about football at this level was the emphasis on details. Of course, high school and high-level college play was about attention to specifics, but it was nothing like I experienced in the pros. When a coach instructed you to cut at just such an angle, he didn't mean approximately or roughly. He meant exactly—forty-five degrees, ninety degrees, what have you. When handing off the ball to a running back, the ball was to be placed just so to allow the runner to gain maximum control without having to slow down or alter his pace. The practices, plays, and repetitions all focused on the specific details of execution. As I said, it was like nothing I had ever experienced before.

If you're wondering, that's why professional teams refer to practice plays as reps. The word—short for repetitions—really means something at this level. Before you can play and win in this league, you need to have every possible detail down to the point where you merely execute it. You don't have time to think about it or remind yourself, *Oh, right, I'm supposed to do it this way.* It's mental memory but also muscle memory. Ideally, things happen as automatically as possible. The only way to achieve that high level of consistency is by practicing the plays and the various movements over and over again.

ONE OF THE FIRST THINGS I CAME TO APPRECIATE ABOUT FOOTBALL AT THIS LEVEL WAS THE EMPHASIS ON DETAILS.

As a player who had come to be known as a great improviser, I was learning that amazing spur-of-the-moment plays are possible only after the details have been practiced over and over and executed properly. There's improvisation, but not always as much as you might assume. Watch for it the next time you're taking in a game. The flow of a play will continue to a certain point, which allows great players the opportunity to take it from there with their own skills.

Despite its obvious value, in professional sports it's no surprise that not everyone likes practice. For some, the routine and repetition become boring and frustrating— practice can seem to go on forever, what with walk- throughs, running the same patterns, throwing the same sorts of passes over and over, hearing the same things repeatedly from the coaching staff. But those who approach it that way have lost their per- spective of practice; it's not

AS A PLAYER WHO HAD COME TO BE KNOWN AS A GREAT IMPROVISER, I WAS LEARNING THAT AMAZING SPUR-OF-THE-MOMENT PLAYS ARE POSSIBLE ONLY AFTER THE DETAILS HAVE BEEN PRACTICED OVER AND OVER AND EXECUTED PROPERLY.

pointless time killing but essential preparation. Although I admit that, for me, practice sometimes becomes a drag, it's essential for success when the game, for lack of a better word, becomes more "fun" with great impro- vised runs and passes thrown with three 350-pound guys bearing down on you. Approach practice with anything less than a focused, committed attitude, and all the fun stuff may never have a chance to take place.

Another essential lesson I learned during my first training camp was the value of asking questions—or, more honestly, of not being afraid to ask questions.

That was always a challenge for me—not because I didn't want to learn but because I've always been somewhat shy. On occasion it's hard for me to speak up, even when a question or issue is pounding inside my head. If you find asking certain questions embarrassing, well, you've got company.

Prior to being drafted, I interviewed with one team that was thinking about selecting me. At first the interview went pretty much as I expected, with questions focused on execution, strategy, work ethic, and other similar topics.

Then all of a sudden the interviewer asked me, "When you hear the word '*woman*,' what's the first thing that pops into your mind?"

I was surprised and had to think about that for a moment. "Respect," I replied.

That was one heck of an awkward moment for me, to put it mildly! At first I couldn't understand why the interviewer would ask a question that, on the surface, had nothing whatsoever to do with football.

But, in giving some thought to it later, I came to understand the value of the question and why I'd been asked it. For one thing, the NFL has struggled and continues to struggle with issues of domestic violence and treatment of women. Our society struggles too. On a practical level, I could see why the team would want to see how a player reacted to that issue when it came up out of the blue. They were looking for an honest answer from the gut—not a reply that someone had time to rehearse and practice, no matter if he truly believed what he was saying.

I also saw that the question had to do with poise. By bringing up a topic that was completely separate from anything else that had been discussed, they were trying to see how I would handle myself, how I could think on my feet in a challenging situation.

For me, it was a valuable lesson in not being afraid to ask questions. Even though I was on the receiving end of the particular inquiry, it must have been somewhat awkward for the interviewer to ask it. It showed me that direct questions need to be asked, no matter how uncomfortable you may feel. It's the only way to learn.

Finally, I learned a lot about patience during my first Texans training camp. As I mentioned earlier, Tom Savage was the Texans' starting quarterback. I understood that completely—he was the veteran; I was the rookie. That's how things should be.

Still, I was in an unfamiliar spot, standing on the sidelines while someone above me on the depth chart was taking the starter's reps. I wasn't used to being in that position, and, although I understood why it was the way it was, I felt frustrated and uncomfortable. But I tried to follow Cam's advice and not let myself get too low.

I knew I had to learn to be patient. No matter who you are, no matter how gifted or talented you happen to be, you have to wait for an opportunity to showcase all that ability. There are very few exceptions to that rule, and I was not one of them. Over the weeks, I began to develop a greater sense of patience, one focused on waiting for the time when I would be given the opportunity to play and hopefully excel. It wasn't my turn yet. In a way, it was a healthy experience, learning how to be patient and prepared no matter how hungry I might be to get in and show what I could do.

Our preseason was hard to read. Tom was the starter in our first game against the Carolina Panthers. I subbed in for him in the second quarter and finished the game, completing fifteen of twenty-five passes and also scoring a touchdown on the ground. We lost 27–17.

The next game was definitely a mixed bag. Although we beat the perennial powerhouse New England Patriots, I played poorly, throwing for only three completions out of ten attempts. Still, I made the most of the experience, learning all I could from watching future Hall of Famer Tom

> NO MATTER WHO YOU ARE, NO MATTER HOW GIFTED OR TALENTED YOU HAPPEN TO BE, YOU HAVE TO WAIT FOR AN OPPORTUNITY TO SHOWCASE ALL THAT ABILITY.

Brady—his execution, his ability to read defenses and make effective adjustments. Watching him play, even for the brief amount of time that starters played in the preseason, was a class unto itself. It seemed like Tom approached the game as though it were the regular season or the playoffs, not preseason. You could see the intensity he put into every play.

We wrapped up the preseason with a 13–0 shutout loss to the Dallas Cowboys. By then, it was clear that the coaching staff had decided on Tom as the starting quarterback when the regular season began.

Even though the preseason produced mixed results for the team, I found it valuable from both a learning and leadership perspective. I was becoming much better at knowing what to look for, knowing what to pay particular attention to, and, just as important, placing myself in various sorts of situations to gauge how I would perform. I watched the players on the field like I had watched the toys I arranged on the living room floor as a boy, seeing where they moved and why and what I would do differently from what I was seeing.

I watched as the various leaders of the team—Tom Savage and Jadeveon Clowney, among others—interacted with the other players. I saw how they motivated them, how they occasionally broke them down to build them back up again. I saw how they expressed leadership through actions as much as words. Like Tom Brady, their approach to leadership in the preseason was as intense and focused as it would be during the regular season.

I began to recognize the constraints of my leadership, given my particular circumstances. I was the rookie, the newcomer, the young guy in the group. Sure, I thought I could lead, but I learned to do so at very specific times when it was appropriate for a young newcomer to speak up. As I'd said back when my team won the state high school championship in Georgia, I was learning it was not my time yet. I would have to wait and develop more to become a complete, fully involved leader.

My commitment to learning and leadership was the right approach. My opportunity came much sooner than I ever expected.

I THOUGHT I COULD LEAD, BUT I LEARNED TO DO SO AT VERY SPECIFIC TIMES WHEN IT WAS APPROPRIATE FOR A YOUNG NEWCOMER TO SPEAK UP.

———

Opening at home against Jacksonville, Tom Savage struggled against the Jaguars' fast, intimidating defense. By halftime we trailed 19–0, and Tom had been sacked six times and lost two fumbles.

During halftime head coach Bill O'Brien pulled me aside. Although they had hoped to bring me along slowly to get a feel for the NFL, Coach said it was obvious we needed some sort of spark before the game spiraled completely out of control. He told me to start warming up. I was taking Tom's place as quarterback.

Since then, a lot of people have asked the obvious question: What did it feel like to get in to your first professional game? On the one hand, I recognized that it was the culmination of all the preparation I had put in, from high school to college to the pros. In a way, even though I was starting on a journey, it also felt as though it was the end of another one.

I was also surprised that, after what felt like so much waiting, this was happening so quickly. To be honest, I really didn't expect to get any significant playing time this early in my rookie season. But it worked to my advantage, in a way. Since everything happened so fast, there wasn't time to get nervous or to overthink it. I just wanted to get out, perform, and show what I could do. My preparation and study would hopefully allow me to execute without having to think too much about it.

I played the remainder of the game against Jacksonville. In the third quarter, I threw my first NFL touchdown, and I finished with 102 passing yards. On the downside, I also threw an interception, and, most important of all, we lost 29–7. Still, it felt great to have my first regular-season playing time under my belt. I was ready to move forward.

My first career start came on September 14, 2017, which also happened to be my twenty-second birthday. We were on the road against the Cincinnati Bengals, and I wasn't about to squander the opportunity to celebrate. On top of 125 passing yards, I also recorded a 49-yard touchdown run in a 13–9 victory—my first as a professional.

Next up was our second game of the year against defending Super Bowl champion New England—only this one counted in the standings.

> MY FIRST CAREER START CAME ON SEPTEMBER 14, 2017, WHICH ALSO HAPPENED TO BE MY TWENTY-SECOND BIRTHDAY.

I was pleased with my performance: 301 passing yards, two touchdowns. But two interceptions and a loss when the game ended—36–33—were definite disappointments. Still, it felt good that we had given the Pats all they could handle.

What was anything but disappointing was watching future Hall of Famer Tom Brady throw for 378 yards, five touchdowns, and no interceptions. It became clear to me that to beat teams the caliber of the Patriots and players like Tom, you had to play as flawlessly as possible. Errors were inevitable, but it was essential to make them as infrequently as possible and with the least amount of damage. I knew I had something to work toward and that it would take both time and focused effort.

That game also pinpointed another step in my leadership development. I started to understand that we as a team weren't completely at the level of the juggernaut that was the Patriots. That, we all knew, would take time to achieve. As I watched our team leaders, I got a sense of that in how they talked with others and carried themselves. Yes, they seemed to say, we're good, but true greatness takes time and patience. An effective leader, I was learning, never expresses impatience with goals that require time.

During week four against the Tennessee Titans, I completed twenty-five of thirty-four passes for 283 yards, four touchdowns, and one interception. I also rushed for 24 yards and one touchdown as we won handily, 57–14. My five total scores tied for the second-most touchdowns scored by a rookie in NFL history behind Gale Sayers's six touchdowns in 1965. I also earned AFC Offensive Player of the Week. Another high.

TRUE GREATNESS TAKES TIME AND PATIENCE. AN EFFECTIVE LEADER, I WAS LEARNING, NEVER EXPRESSES IMPATIENCE WITH GOALS THAT REQUIRE TIME.

That terrific week was offset the following week with a loss to the Kansas City Chiefs, 42–34, on NBC's *Sunday Night Football*. Still, I finished sixteen of thirty-one for 261 yards and five touchdown passes, tying an NFL rookie record for touchdown passes thrown in a single game.

We lost again three weeks later to the Seattle Seahawks, 41–38.

Although I passed for 402 yards and four touchdowns, I also threw three interceptions—an issue I knew I had to work on. My accuracy and decision-making still needed attention, and I focused on both during practice and film study.

Nonetheless, by setting the NFL record for touchdown passes in a calendar month made by a rookie (sixteen), I was named the AFC Offensive Player of the Month and the NFL Offensive Rookie of the Month. (I was honored but also found it kind of funny, remembering Mama Maria's ribbing about me going here and there to collect all these awards.)

Then the season simply fell apart.

The day I received AFC Offensive Player of the Month honors—just four days after the Seattle game—my teammates and I were going through a routine Thursday afternoon training session. The team had invited local members from all the military branches and their relatives as well as the families of players and staff, so there was a larger audience than we usually had for these sorts of everyday drills. Given my award-winning performance the past several weeks, I felt as though a lot of eyes were watching every move I made.

Unfortunately, I gave them more to watch than anyone ever could have expected—myself in particular.

As I went around the right end during a run-through of a play we had practiced dozens of times before, my right knee gave way under me. I fell to the ground without even being touched. At the time it seemed like the most innocent thing imaginable. I felt no pain, nothing out of the ordinary. It was as though I had simply slipped.

As I left the field, I assured the team doctors there was nothing to worry about. I had just landed in a weird way that caused my knee to lock. I wasn't trying to hand them a line. My knee felt fine—totally normal.

But it was anything but normal. After some preliminary evaluation, the doctors insisted on a complete examination. When the results came back, I was stunned. An MRI confirmed that I had torn my ACL—again. My season was done.

Following surgery, I was looking at eight to nine months of rehab. I had been through this before at Clemson—beginning a year as a backup, later named the starter, only to suffer a torn ligament that pulled an entire season out from under me. It was gut-wrenching and all too familiar.

The first thing I did after hearing this was call my family back in Georgia. Mom's reaction was predictable.

"Deshaun, are you okay?" she asked.

"Yes, Mom. I'm really upset."

"Honey, take your time. We've been through this before."

She said that several times more in our conversation. It was just what I needed to hear.

Next, I spoke with my agent. David was very encouraging, urging me to take things one step at a time and not to be overwhelmed by disappointment and frustration. He, too, reminded me that I had overcome a similar situation before.

I HAD BEEN THROUGH THIS BEFORE AT CLEMSON—BEGINNING A YEAR AS A BACKUP, LATER NAMED THE STARTER, ONLY TO SUFFER A TORN LIGAMENT THAT PULLED AN ENTIRE SEASON OUT FROM UNDER ME. IT WAS GUT-WRENCHING AND ALL TOO FAMILIAR.

I knew this was just another low, and I tried not to let it get me down. I determined not to let my injury keep me from contributing to the team, so I decided it was time to study film—and study it with a particularly strong commitment. I reviewed Sunday's game plan against the Indianapolis Colts to see if I could identify anything that might be valuable. The next morning I joined the team at practice, offering to help Tom Savage—the veteran I'd replaced during the season opener—in any way I could.

Even though I couldn't play for the rest of the year, I knew I had to do what I could to be of service to the team. While I couldn't physically take part in practices and games, I still had something to contribute. I wasn't about to ignore any opportunity to continue to serve. In that sense, my injury didn't compromise my commitment in the least; if anything, it broadened it, since I had to be constantly watching for opportunities to contribute other than on the playing field itself. I was learning what it meant to be a leader who was always willing to serve.

I also knew that I had a role in how the team reacted to my injury. I remember watching a television analyst describe how the Texans needed to handle their emotional response to what had occurred. While my injury was discouraging, my teammates and I had to direct our attention to the remainder of the season and deal with the reality of the situation. I knew I had to contribute in every way possible to making sure my teammates' disappointment at my injury didn't impact their attitude moving forward.

WHILE I COULDN'T PHYSICALLY TAKE PART IN PRACTICES AND GAMES, I STILL HAD SOMETHING TO CONTRIBUTE.

My teammate and star defensive lineman J. J. Watt set the tone when he tweeted: "Minor setback for a major comeback. We've all seen what's possible, can't wait to see what's next. With you every step of the way [No.] 4."[2]

I had a lot of disappointment and—yes—anger at having sustained a season-ending injury, but I tried to keep Cam Newton's advice in mind. One thing that helped was realizing that even though my injury was a very big deal for me and my team, I was not the only person in Houston who was having a tough time.

Some were dealing with far worse.

Not long before the start of the 2017 season, Hurricane Harvey devastated Houston and much of the Gulf Coast. The storm killed sixty-eight people and caused about $125 billion in damages. I knew of three ladies who worked in the Texans' practice facility cafeteria who, from what I had heard, had lost pretty much everything they owned in the hurricane. What I was going through now was nothing compared with what those three ladies had to deal with. It was a reminder of the lesson I had learned during my mom's battle with cancer: however challenging my situation was, there was always somebody else who needed help and support more than I did. It was important to keep looking around me and not merely focus on myself.

Because I came from a background where we had little, I knew what it felt like to struggle with deprivation. In the case of the three cafeteria ladies, though, it had been so sudden, so cruel. Scarcity came like a thief who

HOWEVER CHALLENGING MY SITUATION WAS, THERE WAS ALWAYS SOMEBODY ELSE WHO NEEDED HELP AND SUPPORT MORE THAN I DID.

had broken into their homes and taken everything of value to them, including the house itself. Despite that, they and others continued to report to work, some as early as 4:30 a.m., to make sure a team of professional athletes—men essentially playing a boy's game—were properly fed.

The reality of the tragedy those three ladies had suffered seemed out of proportion with fifty-some wealthy athletes downing the calories they needed to perform.

So I decided to do something about it. One morning I giggled self-consciously as I carried three ribbon-wrapped envelopes into the cafeteria. The three women who had lost everything were standing to one side. I handed each of them an envelope with a check for a third of my first NFL game paycheck.

"For what you all do for us every day and never complain, I really appreciate y'all, so I wanted to give my first game check to y'all to help y'all out in some type of way," I told them. "Hopefully, that's good and that can get you back on your feet. And anything else y'all need, I'm always here to help."

Tears streamed down the women's faces as we all hugged. It was as rewarding a moment as any I've ever had in my life. I was focused on what I had and what I could offer to those who had less. Cameras rolled to push the experience into the viral world of television and the internet. I had resisted that part at first because I had wanted to do this in a low-key way. But the public relations people insisted because they knew that spreading the word would lead other people to reach out and help hurricane victims too.

And it worked. Other members of the team stepped up and made donations to help the ladies get back on their feet. On a larger scale, my teammate J. J. Watt spearheaded a fundraising effort, raising tens of millions of dollars to help rebuild hundreds of homes, childcare centers, and after-school programs throughout the Houston area. I'd always admired J. J.'s character and leadership, and his efforts toward hurricane relief made me even prouder to call him my teammate.

But still there was the issue of my injury. As we closed out the 2017–18 season, I committed to regaining my health so I could be fully prepared for the next season.

I had plenty of time to think about that good advice Cam Newton had given me as I worked to get back into shape, and I realized that his wisdom was really all about balance. I try to maintain that sense of balance in everything I do.

For instance, as a professional athlete, I understand that many elements go into being a successful NFL quarterback. With that in mind, I try to strike a balance in my training, not focusing on any one aspect of my play but giving every skill due attention. It's helped me become a better, more well-rounded athlete overall.

I try to do the same in my personal life. Although it can be difficult with the schedule of a professional athlete, I try to strike a balance between the various people and activities outside of football. Naturally, family is often at the top of the list, but so too are friends, activities that I enjoy, my faith, and work in the community. I try to make it so that no one area suffers from a lack of attention because of undue focus on something else.

Thinking about my life in terms of balance has helped me make better decisions and respond to unforeseen circumstances too. If I'm faced with a problem, I try to take the time to slow down and consider every aspect of the situation. I think: *What can I do to address the problem? What's outside of my control? What's the best possible outcome? What's the worst?*

By prompting myself to move beyond merely reacting and, instead, weighing every aspect of what's going on around me, chances are good that I'm more balanced in my approach to the situation. And that leads to better decision-making.

I've developed a way to help me maintain the sort of balance that leads to good choices. It took a while to get a handle on it, but now I try to see myself from a third-person perspective, as though some impartial outsider is watching what I do and offering suggestions for improvement. This allows me to make changes without feeling bad about them or getting down on myself for what I see as weakness or a stupid mistake.

> AS SOMEONE ONCE TOLD ME ABOUT BALANCE, "IF YOU'RE TOO BIG FOR THE SMALL MOMENTS, YOU'LL BE TOO SMALL IN THE BIG MOMENTS."

Maintaining balance means you are able to keep your head while everyone around you is losing theirs. As someone once told me about balance, "If you're too big for the small moments, you'll be too small in the big moments."

In other words—never get too high and never sink too low.

PASS IT ON

- Think back to a time that was particularly stressful. How did you handle it? Were you able to maintain your composure, or did you get caught up in the emotion of the moment? Did you feel a sense of balance, of not getting too excited or too disappointed if things did or didn't go your way?

- Do you have a strategy for balancing the various responsibilities and stresses in your life? How do you think you do at managing it?
- Why do you think it's important to not let yourself focus too much on either extreme highs or extreme lows? How do you find the middle ground?

YOUR CHALLENGE

When you next confront a tense situation or some similar challenge, pay attention to how you react. Work to keep your focus and perspective. It may not be perfect, but the more you work at always having a sense of balance, the better you will be, even in the most challenging circumstances.

THE DESHAUN WATSON FOUNDATION

Helping those women in the cafeteria felt good—so good that I knew I wanted to find a way to help others more regularly. Happily, with my position in sports and the community as a whole, I've been blessed to make that ambition come alive in a rather big fashion.

In early October 2019, I announced the launch of my charitable organization, the Deshaun Watson Foundation. The nonprofit is dedicated to the support of families and young people in underserved communities.

The foundation focuses on four key elements:

1. **Housing:** The organization will offer rent and mortgage assistance for families who need help to find a safe, healthy place to call home.
2. **Education:** The foundation will provide college scholarships and other forms of financial assistance to qualified and deserving students. The organization will also target financial assistance and support to other types of schools and educational programs to better prepare young people for the professional and personal challenges of adulthood.
3. **Health:** The Deshaun Watson Foundation will offer financial and other forms of support for families and children confronted with life-changing medical situations. Just as important, the foundation will assist with offering and promoting various forms of preventative health care.
4. **Other Charitable Causes:** The foundation will also identify and support other initiatives benefiting families and children.

Going down this list, it's easy to see why this foundation's activities mean so much for me. Given my life-changing experience with Habitat for Humanity, I was determined to make housing a cornerstone of the foundation's activities. So, too, the many benefits and blessings I received through an amazing education at Clemson University made educational support of all sorts a vital aspect of the organization.

Lastly, my mom's struggle with cancer ensured that health care would also serve a prominent role in the foundation. If I can help even one family avoid or better deal with the horror that is cancer, I will feel both blessed and honored.

As I learned through the challenges and struggles of my life, a leader always makes certain to give back and put others ahead of him- or herself. In my case, I'm able to do it on a fairly significant scale, but no matter the circumstances, we can all benefit and grow as leaders if we look to put others ahead of our own goals and interests.

Looking to become involved? Check out the Deshaun Watson Foundation at https://www.deshaunwatsonfoundation.org for further information and opportunities to donate or participate in foundation activities and events.

LEARNING TO THINK AS THE UNDERDOG

HAS ALLOWED ME TO TAKE CRITICISM

AND DOUBT THAT OTHERS PLACE ON ME

AND REFRAME IT AS INSPIRATION

TO WORK EVEN HARDER.

CHAPTER 7

IGNORE THE DOUBTERS, FORGIVE THE HATERS

When you're an injured professional athlete, outside doubt can smother you. *Can he come back? Will he be the same? Will he have the confidence to do the same things he used to do?*

At the start of the 2018–19 season, there was widespread concern about my ability to come back from a season-ending injury the prior year. I don't fault anyone who felt doubtful. Sports history is littered with tragic stories of athletes who suffered similar injuries that hindered or effectively ended their careers. Think Joe Theismann, Gale Sayers, and countless others.

But I had been through this before. I knew what I had to do. And I pursued rehabbing my injury with the level of commitment necessary to return to peak playing condition. I owed it to myself to do everything possible to return to playing shape, but I also owed it to others—my teammates, the Texans organization, and the city of Houston. Thinking about all the people depending on you strengthens your commitment and motivation to work all that much harder.

> I OWED IT TO MYSELF TO DO EVERYTHING POSSIBLE TO RETURN TO PLAYING SHAPE, BUT I ALSO OWED IT TO OTHERS—MY TEAMMATES, THE TEXANS ORGANIZATION, AND THE CITY OF HOUSTON.

It was largely a matter of separating the external doubt from my own inner confidence. It may seem a bit blunt, but, occasionally, great leaders have to completely ignore those around them and instead listen only to themselves. It's not so much a question of dismissing others' concerns but instead focusing on what you know, what you feel, and how that can counter the doubts and misgivings of others.

After I underwent surgery in November 2017 to repair my torn ACL, the doctors and training staff mapped out a comprehensive multiweek program to build the knee back up in terms of strength and flexibility—and, at the same time, to reinforce my confidence that the knee would, in fact, perform as it had prior to the injury. Both physical and psychological strength were essential.

The overall rehab environment helped a great deal. In a somewhat strange way, even though I was working to recover from a serious injury, I enjoyed the atmosphere. I was around a lot of other guys working on their own rehab, and each of us tried to make the others better, contributing to the energy of the overall group. Don't misunderstand, it wasn't competitive—when you're competing, you're trying to beat someone else—but the level of commitment and intensity upped everyone's game. We all fed off that energy and worked that much harder. Every one of us wanted to be the first one to be healthy and back on the field.

I approached my healing a little bit differently than other guys did. While some players' reactions to a serious physical issue can range from teeth-gritting frustration to a feeling of utter futility, I was pretty matter-of-fact about my injury. Having been through something like this before helped, but still, I simply knew what would be necessary to get me back on the field in the very best condition possible. It was an emotional time, but I was determined not to get caught up in that emotion. Keeping my focus clear and calm reinforced my commitment to do what was necessary.

Many people around me seemed surprised by my attitude, that I could approach the entire challenge so calmly. Again, while I had been through injuries before, my faith and motivation were so strong that there was no room for doubt in my mind. For me, the thought of not being able to come back completely from the injury was simply unimaginable.

I also maintained a sense of balance, of not getting too discouraged or unduly optimistic. I approached my rehab like it was just business as usual. As I'd said to Roddy White when I was an Atlanta Falcons ball boy, I was just out on the grind.

Fortunately, things began to improve quickly. Not long after I started the rehab program, I was cleared to ditch the crutches I was using to get around. In time, my knee became strong enough to remove the

> WHILE I HAD BEEN THROUGH INJURIES BEFORE, MY FAITH AND MOTIVATION WERE SO STRONG THAT THERE WAS NO ROOM FOR DOUBT IN MY MIND.

knee brace. I began to walk more and more normally with every passing day.

The next step was beginning to run again, a goal I knew I had to be patient about. Given the severity of my injury, that would only come with time and work. But I was able to run faster and more confidently as I progressed. Eventually, I was able to participate in everything except 11-on-11 team drills. From the coaching and medical staffs' standpoint, those drills were just too risky for any player coming back from a significant injury.

———

By the time we hit the opening of training camp that summer, I knew I was ready to take part in everything the team wanted me to do. Even on the very first day, my knee felt so good that I was able to direct my attention to practice without worrying about any physical problems or weaknesses. I was able to look forward, with not even a single glance back at what had happened only a few months before. From a physical standpoint, it was as though the injury had never happened.

But the doubters were concerned about issues other than the health of my knee. Since we had finished the previous season tied for dead last in our division with a dismal 4–12 record, many prognosticators and pundits gave us little chance to make a dent in the competitive AFC South. In their minds, there were simply too many question marks, too many uncertainties. In particular, they pointed to a bleak 1–7 record in road games, something that many of them didn't see us improving on.

I certainly didn't feel that way and neither did my teammates, and hearing all the doubt and concern outside of our locker room merely boosted our confidence and motivation. As we saw it, if someone doubts you and you feel a sense of doubt yourself, you're basically agreeing with them. Like the old saying goes, nobody can make you feel inferior without your consent.

A leader is skilled at tuning out doubters as much as possible and encouraging others to do the same. That's not to suggest ignoring legitimate concerns and issues but, rather, incorporating them into a plan and mindset to address them. Legitimate doubt can be helpful if you use it to your advantage.

> IF SOMEONE DOUBTS YOU AND YOU FEEL A SENSE OF DOUBT YOURSELF, YOU'RE BASICALLY AGREEING WITH THEM. LIKE THE OLD SAYING GOES, NOBODY CAN MAKE YOU FEEL INFERIOR WITHOUT YOUR CONSENT.

Tom Brady helped me really understand that. I've talked to Tom a number of times over the years. Not only do I enjoy the conversations, but I always come away from them with something of value. One comment he made to me seemed particularly appropriate as we approached a new season:

Always feel like you're the underdog.

Tom is a six-time Super Bowl champion, and at first it was hard to believe that he could honestly ever see himself as an underdog, no matter the competition. But he really does. It might be fueled by some critic in the media or trash talk from the opposition, or, against all logic, he may simply convince himself that the team he's going up against has the upper hand. But it really helps Tom, and when I started to put it into practice myself, I understood why.

When you see yourself as the underdog, you recognize that you can never get too comfortable. It means never underestimating your opponent, never telling yourself that you've worked hard enough. Having an underdog mentality is never letting anyone outwork you, never losing sight of what some other competitor might be doing to try to get on top. Learning to think as the underdog has allowed me to take criticism and doubt that others place on me and reframe it as inspiration to work even harder.

WHEN YOU SEE YOURSELF AS THE UNDERDOG, YOU RECOGNIZE THAT YOU CAN NEVER GET TOO COMFORTABLE.

As I like to put it, underdogs are always looking up, never down. And from a leadership standpoint, a gifted leader encourages that attitude in those around him or her. An underdog's hunger grows and becomes more powerful when more people share an underdog mindset.

The 2018–19 season turned out to be one heck of a roller-coaster ride. We lost our first three regular-season games—two, as the naysayers had speculated, on the road against New England and Tennessee. Then the New York Giants came to Houston and bested us on our home field. It was a discouraging beginning.

My play was admittedly sloppy, as I threw an interception in each of the three games. Even though I was confident in my health, it still didn't feel as though I was fully back to 100 percent. Although I tried not to pay attention, it was impossible to completely ignore the critics who began to suggest my rookie season was just another flash in the pan. Once again I forced myself to focus on my own confidence in what I knew I could do.

An 0–3 record to start the season left us with less than a 3 percent chance of making the playoffs. Only five of the 173 teams that had started a season 0–3 since 1980 had recovered to go on to postseason play. The numbers were ominous.

But they also played into the importance of an underdog mindset. With an 0–3 record, we didn't have to convince ourselves that we were underdogs so far as our chances of making it to postseason play. We were underdogs, and that merely fueled our commitment.

I knew I had to step it up, as did all my teammates. We all had to rise to the challenge. And that's just what we proceeded to do.

After our dismal beginning, we rallied for a nine-game winning streak, placing us at the top of the AFC South division, squarely in contention for a first-round bye. We started with a road win against division rival Indianapolis, overcoming a four-touchdown performance by quarterback Andrew Luck. Then we beat in-state rival Dallas in an exciting overtime game. We knew we were on our way.

Still, there were physical challenges. Even though we won both games, the Cowboys and Buffalo Bills pounded me to the point that my lungs deflated in my chest. Unable to withstand the air pressure of flying, I had to take a bus to the next game in Jacksonville to give my lungs time to repair themselves. I kind of felt like I was back in high school, but medically speaking, thirteen hours on a bus was the only safe way to travel.

But with two more wins against Buffalo and Jacksonville, we were sitting at the top of our division. Even better, we had put together our first four-game winning streak in several years.

My own play rebounded. A highlight of the year came in week eight, when I threw for five touchdowns in a win over Miami. My teammates' play also improved, particularly in our run defense.

An emotional win came in week twelve, when we avenged our loss to Tennessee earlier in the year. We dedicated the victory to Bob McNair, the owner and founder of the Texans, who had died that week at age eighty-one after a long battle with skin cancer.

The win was meaningful for all of us. The McNair family was responsible for bringing professional football back to Houston. On a more personal level, the McNairs reached out to my family after I was drafted. They knew my mother's own history with cancer, and I appreciate more than I can say the time they took to connect with her.

I believe Bob McNair is in heaven, watching down on our team. We never want to disappoint him.

———

I focused on improving my overall performance during the 2018–19 season. Working with Coach O'Brien, I looked to boost my involvement in the team to include more than my own play. I began to understand how a certain receiver's skill set can exploit particular cornerbacks. I learned how certain throws can disrupt coverage patterns and what might cause defensive backs to break from planned routes. I embraced the wisdom of knowing when it made sense to try a challenging throw or run and when it was more prudent to run out of bounds and start with a clean slate. My perspective was maturing.

I was also growing as a leader. As I mentioned earlier, when I was a rookie, I had to be really careful about choosing my spots to express leadership. Instead of seeming like someone eager to contribute, I might have come off as an inexperienced know-it-all. But now, with more experience under my belt

WITH MORE EXPERIENCE UNDER MY BELT AND A GREATER FAMILIARITY WITH MY TEAMMATES, I COULD BE MORE VISIBLE AS A LEADER. IT WAS MY TIME TO DO SO.

and a greater familiarity with my teammates, I could be more visible as a leader. It was my time to do so.

I strove to build a pervasive sense of belief in myself, my teammates, and the strategy mapped out by the coaching staff. That belief went beyond mere confidence. Players such as Tom Brady and Aaron Rodgers fill those around them with absolute certainty that they will help their team win. The other players don't have to reason that out or look for evidence—they just believe it to be true. That was the sort of mindset and attitude I was looking to foster as a servant leader. I wanted to be the person others turned to when critical outcomes were on the line.

Still, the last few games of the regular season were hardly things of beauty. After losing at home to the Indianapolis Colts—due in large part to yet another amazing performance by Andrew Luck—we managed to squeak by the New York Jets on a fourth-quarter touchdown. After a last-second loss to the Philadelphia Eagles and a workmanlike win at home against Jacksonville, there were still plenty of skeptics who doubted we would get very far in the postseason.

> I WANTED TO BE THE PERSON OTHERS TURNED TO WHEN CRITICAL OUTCOMES WERE ON THE LINE.

Our first game was a wild card rematch with the Colts and Luck, who had dominated us just a few weeks prior. Despite playing on our home field, we lost the game 21–7, our fewest points of the season.

After Indianapolis established a three-touchdown lead by the end of the first half, we managed to score with 10:57 left in the game on a 6-yard touchdown pass to rookie Keke Coutee. But we continued to struggle. Indianapolis running back Marlon Mack scorched us for 148 yards on the ground. It was the first time all year that our defense allowed more than 100 yards in the game by any one runner.

We were also unable to capitalize when opportunities presented themselves.

With regard to the frustrating level of our play, one particular series stands out in my mind. On a fourth-and-1 at the Indy 9-yard line, I missed badly when trying to connect with wide receiver DeAndre Hopkins at the back of the end zone. In retrospect, I could have easily run for a first down but instead chose to go for broke.

The experience reminded me of all that I had yet to learn.

"The Colts started off faster than us, played better than us, made more plays than us," I said after the game in an interview. "It was a lack of execution on our part. Our communication was a little off. It was tough, but I'm going to keep my chin up and my heart light and go to work this off-season. God willing, we'll have another chance next year. This season had a lot of ups and downs. We made a run. It didn't end the way we wanted it to end, but the future is bright for this organization."[1]

I meant every word.

That's because there were so many positives to the season, despite the naysayers who had dogged us throughout. I played all but one snap. I played through a collapsed lung and a broken rib suffered in a victory over Dallas. We managed to win eleven games despite a rash of other injuries (our second and third receivers missed a combined total of nineteen games, and other key players were also out for significant stretches). During our nine-game winning streak, we won five of those games by seven points or fewer, proof that we had it within us to excel under pressure.

As for myself, over the course of the

DURING OUR NINE-GAME WINNING STREAK, WE WON FIVE OF THOSE GAMES BY SEVEN POINTS OR FEWER, PROOF THAT WE HAD IT WITHIN US TO EXCEL UNDER PRESSURE.

season I threw for 4,165 yards and twenty-six touchdowns. I completed 68.3 percent of my throws and compiled a 103.1 passer rating, averaging 8.2 yards per pass. I also rushed for 551 yards and five touchdowns.

But one of the most memorable moments of the season in terms of my commitment to developing as a servant leader came off the field.

Not long after the regular season began, an East Texas school superintendent took to Facebook to criticize a decision I had made in the early season loss to Tennessee. We had the ball at midfield with seventeen seconds remaining, and I managed to complete a 31-yard pass to DeAndre Hopkins. However big the gain, time ran out as we tried to run another play.

In retrospect, I realized that my instincts took over when making the play that ended our chance for a comeback. At the time, with no time-outs remaining and Tennessee guarding the sidelines to prevent our stopping the clock, it seemed to me that our only chance was a long gain and, hopefully, enough time for another play.

That didn't sit well with Lynn Redden, then superintendent of the Onalaska Independent School District, who remarked on the *Houston Chronicle*'s Facebook page: "That may have been the most inept quarterback decision I've seen in the NFL. When you need precision decision-making you can't count on a black quarterback."[2]

Redden thought he had sent a private message but instead posted the comments publicly.

The day after, he told the *Chronicle* that he wished he had never made those comments. Still, he added: "Over the history of the NFL, they have had limited success."[3]

They.

Coach O'Brien exploded, calling the remarks ignorant and idiotic. But as Cam Newton had warned me, you'll always have haters—people who will try to tear you down simply because it's what they do. So I decided to take a different approach.

When a reporter asked me about the comment, I responded, "That's on him. May peace be with him. I worry about me, so I'm not worried about what he has to say."

The superintendent resigned shortly thereafter.

Admittedly, forgiving the hater wasn't easy. It would have been easy—even understandable—for me to have fired off a response to the comments. But the more I thought about it, the more I realized that responding in anger would accomplish nothing except for making me upset. Further, I saw that it was a leadership opportunity, a chance to keep things in perspective and rise above short-term emotions.

Looking back, was I surprised to find that such remarks still litter our society? Not really. We all say things we wish we hadn't said. And no matter how far we believe we have advanced as human beings, false stereotypes die hard. We all have a tendency to seek out scapegoats rather than look for genuine solutions based on facts and respect. We focus on searching for someone or something to blame instead of working constructively together.

I feel that one of my responsibilities as a leader is to do what I can to discredit and tear down stereotypes of all sorts. The comment made by the school superintendent is just one example of those stereotypes. Despite his feelings on the matter, there are many gifted quarterbacks who also happen to be African Americans.

In 2018, prompted by this incident, my quarterback coach Quincy Avery put together a conference to examine the challenges of being a black quarterback—not just from a physical standpoint but also from the perspective of how others view our skill set.

While outright racism like the school superintendent showed is becoming less common, many black quarterbacks have nonetheless been pigeonholed as limited. For instance, many people still see us as "run first, pass second" athletes, something I mentioned earlier.

I FEEL THAT ONE OF MY RESPONSIBILITIES AS A LEADER IS TO DO WHAT I CAN TO DISCREDIT AND TEAR DOWN STEREOTYPES OF ALL SORTS.

That's certainly not how I see myself, and I said so in that conference.

"I love sitting in the pocket. I love making those decisions," I told the group. "Anyone asks me if I'd rather run for a touchdown or throw, I'm going to choose pass. But sometimes I feel like I get labeled as a running quarterback a lot more than passing."

I believe the environment is changing for the better, particularly when you have so many young, gifted African American quarterbacks such as Russell Wilson, Patrick Mahomes, and Lamar Jackson establishing themselves as talented, complete football players. But change takes time, and all the more so when the issue at hand is subtler than more visible forms of stereotyping.

I've learned that leaders not only work to correct that sort of counterproductive thinking but also look for it when it occurs in quiet ways. For me, the best strategy is to go out each and every week and play the best, most complete game that I possibly can. The more examples I can give, and the more others can give, the more discredited the narrow, outdating thinking and attitudes become.

These days when I face criticism or doubts, I try to maintain a long-term perspective and focus on the bigger picture so I won't be

I BELIEVE THE ENVIRONMENT IS CHANGING FOR THE BETTER, PARTICULARLY WHEN YOU HAVE SO MANY YOUNG, GIFTED AFRICAN AMERICAN QUARTERBACKS SUCH AS RUSSELL WILSON, PATRICK MAHOMES, AND LAMAR JACKSON ESTABLISHING THEMSELVES AS TALENTED, COMPLETE FOOTBALL PLAYERS.

discouraged by short-term missteps. I also try to learn from my mistakes as well as those made by others. I try to take the time to minimize blame and finger-pointing and, instead, focus on what I can learn. I try to think of these as educational experiences.

Most of all, I try to stop and consider all the love that's in my life, no matter what is going on in the moment. Because not everyone is going to love what I do, but I am surrounded by love in my life, and that makes it so much easier to stop listening to the voices of the doubters and listen to the voices of those who care about me instead.

PASS IT ON

- Have you seen or experienced a subtle form of negative stereotyping? Where did it occur and how? Did others around you notice it as well? Did anyone say or do something? What happened?
- Consider the stereotypes you harbor about other people. Think about how you express them. What steps can you take to eliminate that sort of thinking in your words and actions?
- Have you had an experience of blaming someone else unjustifiably, or, by the same token, have you been blamed by someone else

for something that simply wasn't reasonable? If you're the guilty party, did you take the time to apologize to the other person? If you were the one receiving the blame, how well were you able to keep it in context, to not take the criticism too seriously or personally? Do you have a strategy to remind yourself that we are all flawed and we all make mistakes?

YOUR CHALLENGE

Make a list of all the people and things that you genuinely love. Then say why you love them. Make this a living list—keep adding new types of loves as well as reasons for loving them. Additionally, the next time someone expresses doubt about you or what you're doing—or, more unfortunately, says something that you find offensive—try wishing that person well regardless. It's a really liberating feeling!

A LEADER HAS TO BE ABLE TO WITHSTAND THE STORMS THAT COME WITHOUT BEING KNOCKED OVER.

CHAPTER 8

BEND, DON'T BREAK

I grew up in the South, where there are palm trees pretty much everywhere. To some, they're funny looking, all tall and skinny with great big leaves on top that make the trees look like they're about to fall over. They're gangly and strange. As I got older, I noticed something interesting about them. When big storms would roll through, we'd end up with downed power lines because trees would fall on them. Sometimes you'd see these big old oak and maple trees that, despite their giant root systems, had snapped like splinters, but I noticed that the palm trees never seemed to share the same fate.

I moved to Houston shortly before Hurricane Harvey, and after the storm, the same thing was true there as well. The city of Houston and surrounding areas were littered with broken limbs and trees that had been completely uprooted, but most of the palm trees had survived reasonably intact.

Then I learned the secret. Palm trees aren't actually made of wood but of a spongy material that allows the trunk to bend over in the wind. They're more closely related to grasses than regular trees, and they twist in the same way that a grass blade bends when the wind hits it. That flexibility is what makes them so good at withstanding strong winds; when a storm comes, a palm tree will bend but not break.

A leader, likewise, has to be able to withstand the storms that come without being knocked over. Leaders have to be able to bend but not break.

This ability to bend but not break is at the heart of the success I've enjoyed throughout my life, and the same can be true for you, regardless of where you came from, what you do, and where you hope to go. Bending but not breaking is really about resiliency—the ability and commitment to come back after some sort of mistake, problem, or even outright tragedy. That's what makes a leader.

Every one of us is going to experience failure or discouragement sometime in our lives. We're all going to have to deal with disappointment. Unfortunately, all of us will have to cope with some type of tragedy—even a devastating one.

BENDING BUT NOT BREAKING IS REALLY ABOUT RESILIENCY— THE ABILITY AND COMMITMENT TO COME BACK AFTER SOME SORT OF MISTAKE, PROBLEM, OR EVEN OUTRIGHT TRAGEDY.

We can't change this. But what we can change is how we react to those issues and problems. We can develop the strength to continue moving forward, learning from the experiences, and, as a result, becoming stronger and more confident. That's the goal of the servant leader—to endure hardship, to become a better person as a result, and to encourage others to do the same.

One of the first and most powerful examples I experienced of bending but not breaking was my mom's battle with tongue cancer. It was terrifying, and we didn't know how it was all going to turn out. But my mom refused to break. Not only did she keep fighting the disease until she ultimately won, but she made certain that, whatever the outcome, our family wouldn't break as a result. I've never seen a more courageous commitment to bending but not breaking in the face of ominous odds.

As various challenges have come up in my own life, I've reacted differently, depending on the situation, but in the end the challenges haven't broken me. I hope hearing my stories will both comfort and inspire you to better deal with the storms in your life.

One of the most obvious challenges I've faced in my career is the series of injuries I've suffered—often happening at the worst possible times. For instance, my first significant ACL tear couldn't have occurred at a more devastating moment—two games before Clemson's game versus in-state rival South Carolina, a team I had promised Coach Swinney we would never lose to as long as I could stay on the field.

I managed to overcome that pain, keep playing, and help us win that game by focusing on my vow to Coach Swinney. As I've said before, a servant leader's word is his absolute bond—you never say anything you don't fully intend to do, no matter the circumstances. Yes, the injury was painful to play through, and, yes, it did end my season, but I kept my word to my coach, my teammates, and my university. That's all that mattered—then and now. I never came out of that game, and in my mind, that showed I had bent but hadn't broken.

My next experience with developing resiliency had nothing to do with any sort of physical injury, but in many ways it was more painful than any muscle tear or broken bone. The national championship loss to Alabama in early 2016 was one of the most devastating losses I've ever experienced. A lot of that had to do with the setting, with a national title in the balance and millions of people watching on television. There could not have possibly been a bigger, more visible stage. Losing hurts that much more when it's conspicuous.

The loss to Alabama was incredibly tough in and of itself. But what made it all the more difficult for me was my own performance, and not in the way that you might assume. I didn't play poorly—anything but. Throwing for four touchdowns and more than four hundred yards against perhaps the best defense in the country was an achievement of which I was justifiably very proud.

But I still left the field thinking I could have done more—made one more complete pass or audibled a different play. Looking back, it was a powerful lesson: sometimes your greatest disappointments occur not when you fail to perform to your ability but as the result of the nagging feeling that somehow, someway, you could have changed the outcome. I'm not suggesting you beat yourself up but instead stretch your goals and definition of success a bit further.

I recognized my own particular responsibility for the defeat as the team's leader. When you're out in front, it's your job to shoulder much of the accountability, regardless of the outcome. Servant leaders embrace a special sort of joy when their group succeeds—and they also have to cope with an oversized amount of heartache when things don't go their way. It's challenging, but it's all part of the responsibility you take on.

Losing that game was tough, but I had to make sure it didn't break me. Leaning on the support of others was critical in this time. For instance, my friend Cam Newton's thoughts and encouragement were indispensable in helping me regain my mental and emotional balance following our loss. Being a servant leader means being strong when you need to be and seeking out support when you need it. Turning to others is a sign of strength; it shows that you appreciate the help they can give.

Much of learning to bend but not break has to do with how you react to defeat. Always maintain perspective, no matter if it's over the short term or your focus is on long-term goals and dreams. Maintain your emotional and mental balance as much as possible. Make learning from the experience part of your determination not to break.

> BEING A SERVANT LEADER MEANS BEING STRONG WHEN YOU NEED TO BE AND SEEKING OUT SUPPORT WHEN YOU NEED IT.

In my case, I learned to never take a loss lying down. I make it a point to get back to work as soon as possible after a defeat—because if you haven't learned from a loss, it can't make you stronger.

That Alabama game battered me like a storm, but I survived, and I was stronger for it. I decided I had to get to work right away to begin preparing for the next season and, I hoped, another chance at a national championship. Losing that game redoubled my determination for a better result whenever the next time came around.

As you know, that opportunity came in the championship rematch with Alabama the following year.

Coming back from a ten-point deficit late in a game against a vaunted defense certainly showed that I and all my Clemson teammates were capable of continuing to get back up again after being knocked down.

An interesting thing about getting up again when you've been knocked down is that it's habit-forming. Once you realize you are, in fact, that much stronger for the experience, you know you can and will get up again. It becomes part of your DNA. Doing anything else seems out of character, even weird.

Of course, by the time I'd gotten to college, I'd already endured many things that could have broken me. From growing up without a dad to living in government housing to my mom's cancer, I had spent much of my childhood bent against the wind. Because of this early struggle, I was flexible enough not to break when these challenges arose in college. My early years taught me to focus on and appreciate what I had instead of wondering what might have been. I tried to identify the positives in many seemingly hopeless situations.

And because of all the people who had helped me through those times, I wasn't trying to be strong for just myself. Every time I awoke at 5:00 a.m. to get ready for another day of mental and physical challenges, my first thoughts were for my family—my mom, my siblings, and my aunts and uncles. For all that I was trying to achieve personally, I also hoped that my achievements would make their lives better. Bending but not breaking meant moving my thoughts away from just myself and paying attention to others in my life who could benefit from my work and dedication—the lesson my mom had nurtured in me.

> MY EARLY YEARS TAUGHT ME TO FOCUS ON AND APPRECIATE WHAT I HAD INSTEAD OF WONDERING WHAT MIGHT HAVE BEEN.

My rookie season with the Texans challenged me too. By this time, I was getting a little tired of my ongoing struggles to keep my knees healthy. My knee injury that ended my first season with the Texans was particularly frustrating—rather than occurring in the violence of real game conditions, I tore my ACL while making what seemed to be an innocent, completely routine cut during practice. It reminded me that challenges can come anywhere and at any time.

As I came to learn, an injury I'd sustained during my high school playing days back in Gainesville had been misdiagnosed, effectively making me all the more vulnerable to additional injuries moving ahead (my current doctors had the diagnostic resources to identify the past oversight). In a way, that intensified the challenge of bending but not breaking—if the doctors had properly diagnosed my injury when I was in high school, I might have avoided all that happened.

Immediately, I went back to work, studying film, giving my teammates what advice and suggestions I could, and devoting myself to rehab. I also focused on my public image, how teammates and others saw me. I tried to seem happy all the time, in high spirits, confident, and committed. The image I wanted to project was that my injury was just another bump in the road. And for the most part, I truly believed it to be.

Those closest to me knew otherwise. As I rehabbed, I spent a lot of time talking on the phone with Brian, a friend I've known all my life and the one who remembered my role as the Big Bad Wolf in grade school. During one conversation, Brian hesitated a moment before asking me, "This thing really has you down, doesn't it?"

I had to admit that, yes, there were times when my injuries made me feel as depressed as I had ever been in my life.

But I did my utmost not to let it overwhelm me. Acknowledging to myself how I was feeling was essential to my overall health, but I also recognized I had to remain confident and committed. That was how I was able to keep moving forward.

Another element of resiliency is learning to correct mistakes as quickly as possible. It's an important part of leadership, and it's part of how you can survive the storms, but I have to admit that doing so doesn't always make me the most pleasant person to be around.

For instance, my family had come to Houston in September 2019 to watch a game against the Carolina Panthers. It was a disappointing game. I missed on two very makeable but critical throws, and we lost to the Panthers. After the game I was in no mood to socialize, even with my loved ones. They just flew home because they knew full well what the next few hours for me would be like.

ANOTHER ELEMENT OF RESILIENCY IS LEARNING TO CORRECT MISTAKES AS QUICKLY AS POSSIBLE.

First, I took care of the required postgame press conference. Framing the loss as a learning experience, I walked the reporters through everything I had noticed about the Panthers' defense. I wanted them—as well as anyone else who would hear or read about what I had to say—to know how it felt to be on the field and the challenges of having to react quickly and intelligently.

After the conference was over, I reached out to Quincy Avery, the quarterback coach I had worked with since high school. Normally, Quincy comes to Houston every game day to share his notes and feedback, but he wasn't there this time, so I asked him to fly in as soon as possible. Something about my disappointing performance made me need Quincy—right then and there.

Quincy and I immediately watched film of every single play in that game. Then we went out on the field to practice those throws that I knew I should have made but simply hadn't. After a couple of hours, I concluded that my timing was just a bit off, that I was moving in the pocket more than was absolutely necessary.

I knew I had to address those sorts of mistakes at the very first opportunity I had—which, as it happened, was right after the game itself was over. That was how I responded to loss, and it made me a better quarterback.

I think "bend but don't break" is at the heart of what it looks like to me to be a servant leader. You get knocked down, learn from it, and get back up again, stronger than before.

PASS IT ON

- What gives you strength? Is it your faith, your family, your community? How do you tap those resources for your own personal strength?
- How comfortable are you turning to others for support to boost your sense of strength? Do you consider it a true sign of servant leadership? If you feel it's a sign of weakness, what can you do to overcome that damaging form of self-criticism?
- Do you truly value what you have rather than hungering for something else? Are you able to balance the value of the present with a healthy focus on the future? Make a list of what you value in your life today. Keep the list handy, and add to it as new things occur to you.
- Are you able to narrow your sense of focus in a particular situation so you know precisely what you need to do in any given moment? If so, what steps do you follow? Do you stop and carefully think things out, or are your instincts more reliable? The more you practice acting with focus in the moment, the better you will get at it.

- Think about how you come back from failure or disappointment. Are you eager to review what you did as soon as you can, or do you prefer to let the dust settle a little bit before you address what went wrong?

YOUR CHALLENGE

Try bending but not breaking in a couple of ways when looking to rebound from some sort of setback. In one instance, start going over what happened as soon as you can. The next time you deal with failure or adversity, allow some time to pass before you begin your investigation of what went wrong. Over time, see which approach is more effective for you.

THERE'S ALWAYS GOING TO BE SOMEONE BIGGER, FASTER, AND MORE TALENTED THAN ME. I CAN'T DO ANYTHING ABOUT THAT. BUT I CAN ALWAYS CHOOSE TO OUTWORK THAT PERSON.

CHAPTER 9

NEVER STOP PRACTICING,
NEVER STOP LEARNING

Basketball Hall of Famer Larry Bird has talked about some advice from a coach that stayed with him throughout his career. As he was quoted in the *New York Times*: "My coach told me, 'Larry, no matter how much you work at it, there's always someone out there who's working just a little harder—if you take 150 practice shots, he's taking 200.' And that drove me."[1]

That's a principle I've used in my life as well. Phrased another way, there's always going to be someone bigger, faster, and more talented than me. I can't do anything about that. But I can always choose to outwork that person. If I think another quarterback is making 150 practice throws, I'm going to make 200. If he stays an hour after every practice, sign me up for two.

Early in my career with the Texans, columnist John McClain of the *Houston Chronicle* made some very nice comments about my work ethic, praising me for staying after practice and working on off days to improve myself: "I can't overstate how hard rookie QB Deshaun Watson worked in the off-season. Stayed after practice. Worked on days off. What a work ethic!"[2]

When I read what John wrote, all I could say was "It's a lifestyle."[3]

For a servant leader, hard work should be a lifestyle—an ongoing choice that never changes. It should be part of your DNA, as important a part of your personal makeup as anything else. You shouldn't have to put all that much thought into it.

> HARD WORK SHOULD BE A LIFESTYLE— AN ONGOING CHOICE THAT NEVER CHANGES.

Hard work is the best way to position yourself to help those around you succeed. For instance, if I work on a particular type of throw or scheme and really get it down, that's going to help my receivers on their end of the play. Hard work never exists in a vacuum.

Continual practice is also an example to others. When others see you working hard, they're inclined to follow your lead. Again, hard work is pervasive, an attribute that any servant leader wants to encourage others to emulate.

But I haven't limited my conviction to hard work just to the football field. I also carried that commitment into the classroom. By working hard, I was able to finish high school early and graduate from Clemson in three years.

Making a habit of hard work gives you the confidence to rise above the naysayers. When I first decided to complete my Clemson degree in less than the usual four years, I naturally had my share of doubters.

They weren't being nasty or critical for criticism's sake. Instead, given the enormous amount of time and energy required to play high-caliber college football, they just didn't see how it would be possible for me to succeed in that area while graduating well ahead of the usual schedule.

Yet I did just that—through time management, self-sacrifice, and my commitment to hard work. And I gained a fresh wave of confidence in myself. When you achieve something that others are doubtful about, you come out the other side that much more confident—not just in what you achieved but in everything you pursue.

A sign in the Gainesville High School locker room boils the issue down to a simple question: "Did anyone outwork you today?" Every day I try to make sure I can answer truthfully no.

But working hard isn't enough. A leader also has to find new ways to improve his mind and his skills. One semester in college I signed up for a series of American Sign Language courses. Some people joked that, with my reserved personality, I jumped at the chance to take that class just so I didn't have to talk. But truly I loved the challenge of it. Not only was it difficult to get the alphabet down, we were taught to focus on facial expressions—not just the hands—to better understand what someone would be trying to say.

Part of the class also included social events at local restaurants with people from the deaf community. We went to Chick-fil-A, Pizza Hut, and other places a number of times. But the food was not the point. Knowing enough sign language to communicate with someone others might find hard to connect with was incredibly rewarding. It also helped me use and develop different parts of my brain.

It was yet another lesson in leadership. A leader understands that everyone has something to say, everyone has something to contribute. The problem is, some are challenged to get their message across.

Learning sign language and communicating with people for whom communication with the hearing world was difficult showed me the challenge wasn't theirs alone. As a leader, it was also up to me to find a way to connect with them.

———————

As I grow and mature further in servant leadership, I've come to realize that servant leaders never stop being students.

A LEADER UNDERSTANDS THAT EVERYONE HAS SOMETHING TO SAY, EVERYONE HAS SOMETHING TO CONTRIBUTE.

For me, a commitment to learning works hand in hand with all the values and attributes I've discussed throughout this book. From my earliest days in school and on the football field, I've prided myself on my teachability. No matter who or what was doing the teaching, I believed there was always something I could learn.

Obviously, I've been blessed with gifted, passionate teachers throughout my life—Coaches O'Brien, Miller, Perry, and Swinney, not to mention Mrs. Frierson, Mama Maria, and my classroom instructors. I'm grateful beyond words for all they shared and taught me.

Being a committed student also means paying attention to others, regardless of whether they're consciously teaching you or not. For me, that's meant studying the skills and abilities of some of the NFL's greatest quarterbacks—Tom Brady, Aaron Rodgers, Drew Brees, and many others. Not only do I look at their playmaking and decision-making skills; I look at their own paths as students—how they got to be where they are and what learning moments helped push them forward to that level of excellence.

I recently decided to push myself to learn something new and took up the game of chess. I do have my nerdy side, as anyone who knows me will attest to, and this came out in force when I really started to grasp the game. Chess has been a revelation both to my intellectual growth as a leader and also in my performance on the football field.

During the summer of 2019, I was introduced to a performance coach named Seth Makowsky. He consults with a number of organizations and businesses, including Fortune 500 companies, sports teams, airports, hotels, casinos, and investment firms, to help improve performance.

> CHESS HAS BEEN A REVELATION BOTH TO MY INTELLECTUAL GROWTH AS A LEADER AND ALSO IN MY PERFORMANCE ON THE FOOTBALL FIELD.

I told Seth that I wanted to improve my leadership skills in terms of better understanding strategy—how various parts interact and work together. Seth suggested I give chess a try.

The nerd in me shifted into overdrive the very first time I sat behind a chess board. My initial "training" session went on for more than three hours. "[Watson] nerded out," as my quarterback coach Quincy Avery joked to *Bleacher Report*.[4] I wasn't just interested in learning how the individual pieces moved and their strengths and weaknesses; I was captivated by the synergy, how the pieces could work together effectively or, just as easily, against each other. I was fascinated with gifted chess players' ability to plan and execute their strategy many moves in advance.

But my involvement in chess wasn't limited to sitting at a table. I began to introduce chess into my practice on the football field itself. During breaks I would go over to a table where a board was set up. Playing against an opponent—often Seth—I would make a move or two, then get back to practicing.

Not only did the ongoing exposure to chess help me better understand strategy and how to help direct an overall strategy as a leader; it also taught me how to focus my mind. (The popular buzzword these days is *mindfulness*.) I learned not to dwell on unnecessary, unhelpful thoughts. I learned what it meant to be completely focused on a task or a decision at hand.

A football in one hand, a chess piece in the other. How athlete/ nerdy can you get?

Learning doesn't necessarily have to take place when there's a "teacher" present. In fact, a servant leader approaches every experience and situation as a learning experience. That can be everything from a joyous victory on the football field to the most crushing of defeats.

And as I've mentioned before, defeat is the best teacher you could possibly have. In many ways, success can be a false friend. It feels wonderful to win, but winning can also make you complacent—giving you a false sense of safety and confidence.

Losing, on the other hand, can fill you with the resolve to move forward and continue to improve. When you lose, it means someone or something was better than you—more prepared, better positioned to execute. With losing you come face-to-face with what you have to do to avoid that defeat again. You see who or what won and why, and you learn from those examples, however difficult they may be.

A leader understands that losing is rarely permanent, that there are almost always opportunities for victory and redemption. Chess really taught me that principle. For instance, if a player loses an important piece such as a bishop or a rook, it's a setback, but the game isn't necessarily over. By learning from the mistake that led to the loss of a critical piece, you can reap the benefits of losing before the final outcome and, perhaps, come back and win.

> IN MANY WAYS, SUCCESS CAN BE A FALSE FRIEND. IT FEELS WONDERFUL TO WIN, BUT WINNING CAN ALSO MAKE YOU COMPLACENT.

A servant leader is always a dedicated student, understanding that nothing ever stays quite the same. Football is an ideal example. From season to season, from game to game, and even from one quarter to the next, everything is changing—people, situations, emotions. Nothing is identical—except perhaps your determination to learn all you can, no matter who or what is the teacher of the moment.

Every moment is an opportunity to learn, as I see it. And by staying committed to learning, your example shows others the value of their own learning as well.

Even better, the more you pursue learning, the better you get at it. You grow in your ability to retain information and insight and process them. In my case, as a quarterback, I used to be able to keep one or two plays in my head along with a few options. But because of my commitment to learning, I can now handle as many as a half dozen plays at the same time, reviewing them in my head to see which one might work best in a particular situation.

Lastly, being a student reinforces your sense of humility. By committing to ongoing learning at every opportunity, you acknowledge that you can't possibly know it all. You know that physical skills and attributes mean little without the intelligence to execute and coordinate them.

As a servant leader, you never stop growing. And maintaining the mindset of a student is central to that sort of growth.

PASS IT ON

- Ask yourself honestly: Are you a hard worker? How do you define hard work? Is it a matter of giving everything you can or outworking those around you? In your opinion, how important is the value of hard work with regard to obtaining significant goals?
- Would you consider yourself a student, someone who is continually learning? If you do see yourself as a student, do you actively seek out opportunities for learning? Moreover, do you look for learning opportunities that are especially challenging, or are you more comfortable with learning at a slower, less-demanding pace?
- Think about the activities you enjoy. Are they teaching you something, such as focus, patience, flexibility, or determination? Taking what you consider fun to a deeper level can make those activities all the more rewarding.
- Consider taking up an activity or hobby—maybe learning a musical instrument, cooking, gardening, or some other pastime—that you think can offer useful benefits to you as a leader.

YOUR CHALLENGE

Set aside a period of time—at least a day, but ideally longer than that. Pay attention to everything you learn over that time frame. Write down everything that you've learned. At the end of the exercise, look over all that you've learned. Is there a common theme to what you see? Do you recognize any particular value in what you've learned?

HUMILITY MEANS
RECOGNIZING
THAT YOU DON'T
HAVE ALL THE
ANSWERS.

CHAPTER 10

STAY HUMBLE

Anyone who wants to stay humble should do what I had to do just prior to the 2017 NFL Draft.

A few days before my draft, with my future in the NFL still very much up in the air, the fantasy sports company DraftKings sent me out into a Philadelphia park not too far from where the draft was being held. Trailed by a camera crew, I interviewed passersby about who they thought were the top quarterbacks in the upcoming draft.

None of the people I spoke with recognized me. That's where both the fun and the lesson in humility began.

Granted, a few people were familiar with my name. Some people praised me for my mobility and overall skills. And one lady noted that Deshaun Watson should be drafted because he was "cute."

I've always enjoyed talking with people who are that observant!

But I also managed to get an earful. One gentleman said I shouldn't be taken in the first round, questioning my arm strength and ability to throw on the run. I struggled to find a follow-up question after hearing that. Another gentleman said he didn't care about the draft at all and that many high picks would be "selling Christmas trees by December." All I could do was hope that he didn't include me in that group.

Still, it was a lot of fun, and the people I interviewed got a real charge when they were told who was interviewing them (one young lady kept shouting "That's not fair!" when she realized who I was). But it was a real lesson in humility for me. Not only did none of them recognize me, but several were less than complimentary about where I should be taken in the draft.

It was a great experience in learning the value of keeping your feet firmly planted on the ground. Like they used to say way back when: never, ever believe your own press clippings. Instead, pay attention to those who speak plainly without any sort of agenda or reasons for saying flattering things.

FOR ME, THE VIRTUE OF REMAINING HUMBLE IS WHAT TIES ALL THE PRIOR QUALITIES TOGETHER WHEN DEVELOPING AS A SERVANT LEADER.

For me, the virtue of remaining humble is what ties all the prior qualities together when developing as a servant leader.

When you're humble, you focus on what you have, not what you don't. You recognize that we all have our challenges and problems, and, in a spirit of unity, you're eager to reach out and help in any way possible.

When you're humble, you're naturally hardworking. You're not about to take anything for granted. Dedication is a given.

When you're humble, you maintain a sense of balance—the ability to step back and see things as they are without any ego-driven filters or overblown fears. Nothing gets you too high or drops you too low.

When you're humble, you're naturally spiritual. You know that there are forces stronger and more powerful than you, and you welcome them into the choices you make.

When you're humble, you're open-minded. Your thoughts are not cast in stone. You welcome new thoughts, ideas, and observations.

When you're humble, you're observant. You understand that you don't know everything there is to know, and, by remaining observant, you're constantly learning.

Humility comes down to being respectful—of others, of groups and institutions with which you may be associated, of new ideas, and, perhaps most important, of yourself. That's a core characteristic of leadership.

Most of us know what's good for us and what is not. Unfortunately, that clarity can be inadvertently compromised by short-term influences—shortcuts, moral compromises, and other missteps.

Granted, it's human to make mistakes. The trick, particularly for a servant leader, is not to make them too often—and to learn from each and every one.

Humility means recognizing that you don't have all the answers. None of us does. But by putting the values you embrace into practice, you're humbly expressing your confidence that those values may benefit others as well. A servant leader will not and cannot be perfect. Understanding that helps one grow as a leader who both leads others and serves them.

A lot of football players are big-time talkers. I hear them all the time, defensive players across the line telling me how they're coming after me, to get ready for a face full of dirt.

I'm not much of a talker. I'd rather make the play and keep my mouth shut, both before and after. I think that's also an important aspect of being humble. You're humble in the face of both success and failure.

An old saying suggests that many people talk the talk but don't walk the walk. Like other issues I've discussed, a servant leader doesn't have that choice.

That's because servant leaders are judged as much by their actions as they are by their words. And to be a truly effective and inspiring servant leader, you cannot say one thing then do something that runs completely counter to your words. That version of "Do as I say, not as I do" can undermine others' confidence in your commitment and personal integrity.

That's one of the key elements I'm continuing to learn about in my development as a leader. To inspire others to follow you, not only do you need to have values with which they identify and embrace, but you must act on those values as well.

TO BE A TRULY EFFECTIVE AND INSPIRING SERVANT LEADER, YOU CANNOT SAY ONE THING THEN DO SOMETHING THAT RUNS COMPLETELY COUNTER TO YOUR WORDS.

Some people imagine that a leader is someone whose values, priorities, and ideas are cast in stone. After all, a leader has to be strong in his or her convictions. That's certainly true, but by my way of thinking, a leader also has to be exceedingly open-minded. Leaders welcome new ideas, new thoughts, and new perspectives.

Early in my football career, I decided to do all that I could to remain as teachable as possible. As a young player, that wasn't particularly difficult to do. Listening to others with more insight and experience, you naturally want to take in as much as you can. Remaining open-minded is key to doing that. It's also a great way to keep you humble.

I've carried that over into adulthood and my position as a servant leader of my team. I am every bit as eager as I ever was to learn as much as possible and remain open-minded. If I don't do those things, I may miss out on a great deal that would improve my play and my overall contribution to the team.

As I see it, a leader who refuses to be open-minded is displaying a destructive form of arrogance—an assumption of knowing all that needs to be known. If you step back and look at that objectively, you'll see that's pretty much an impossibility. None of us knows everything worth knowing. To suggest otherwise is simply unrealistic.

Further, as a servant leader, failing to keep an open mind also sends a message to those around you. In effect, you may be suggesting that you don't value their thoughts and ideas. You're telling them that, in your mind, they have nothing to contribute. That's hardly a formula to inspire those around you to pursue great things.

I cannot tell you how many times players have returned to a huddle and told me something that they felt I needed to know. For instance, a receiver may point out that a certain type of coverage is breaking down over the middle of the field or that a linebacker is "cheating" as he moves closer to the line of scrimmage. Almost inevitably, they're right, and we as a group benefit accordingly. If a leader dismisses that kind of feedback and insight, your success may suffer, not to mention, once again, you're sending an unstated message to the group that you don't value what they want to contribute. Keep it to yourself, you're essentially telling them.

Open-mindedness is a key component for any servant leader, regardless of the setting. It shows that you value everyone—particularly those eager to share new ideas and thoughts.

Staying humble is also a part of understanding when certain types of leadership are appropriate. As a rookie, I understood the value of taking on my leadership role slowly and carefully, not overstepping my bounds. As I've been on the team longer, I've had to adjust my leadership skills and approach.

For instance, I've tried to take the time to learn what styles of interaction certain players prefer. Some, I've come to realize, like a more intimate, calm, one-on-one environment. Others, believe it or not, embrace the experience of being yelled at in front of the rest of the team. The visibility fires them up.

Ultimately, no matter how I try to convey it, I like to let the others around me know that I value them and that I don't think I'm in a position of greater importance than they are. My goal has always been to lead as well as serve, and I think that emerges when I take the time to approach every player as an individual rather than just another number on a football squad.

I once heard someone say that once we all stop learning, we stop living. By being humble, keeping an open mind, and remaining open to teaching moments, servant leaders can avoid that unfortunate fate and, in so doing, help those around them to do the same.

> MY GOAL HAS ALWAYS BEEN TO LEAD AS WELL AS SERVE, AND I THINK THAT EMERGES WHEN I TAKE THE TIME TO APPROACH EVERY PLAYER AS AN INDIVIDUAL RATHER THAN JUST ANOTHER NUMBER ON A FOOTBALL SQUAD.

PASS IT ON

- What do you think makes a person humble? Do you consider yourself humble? Have you considered what benefits you can receive if you approach things with a humble perspective?
- Think of an experience where you were not particularly humble. How did that make you feel? Did your lack of humility affect the outcome of the situation?
- When you've found yourself in a position of leadership, how do you approach those you lead? Do you see and address them as a group or as individuals who would benefit from a more one-on-one strategy?

YOUR CHALLENGE

The next time you're having a conversation with someone who knows more about a particular topic than you, tell that person how much you appreciate the shared knowledge. Being humble builds both relationships and your own personal store of knowledge.

I OWE SO MUCH OF WHAT
I'VE BECOME IN MY LIFE
TO THOSE COACHES WHO
INVESTED THEIR TIME
AND ENERGY IN ME.

CHAPTER 11

FIND A COACH, BE A COACH

I can't tell you how many times a game that felt like it was slipping away was completely turned around by a few words from a gifted coach.

I remember one game when I repeatedly tried to make long throws. Some connected, but many did not. I had seen the defense—a Cover 2 scheme, meaning a defense in which the safeties play farther back—but continued to try to beat them long. The offense was struggling, and we were losing.

My quarterback coach pulled me aside. "Don't try to hit a home run every time," he said. "You're playing right into their defense by going long. Loosen them up with some intermediate passes."

He was right. Shorter passes lured the safeties closer to the line of scrimmage, opening up the long ball. We came back from a deficit and won the game handily.

Throughout my life I have been blessed to have worked with and benefited from all sorts of gifted coaches.

Some have the word *coach* attached to their names—Coaches Perry, O'Brien, Swinney, just to name a few.

But other coaches who have provided me valuable guidance and insight don't necessarily refer to themselves as coaches—my mom, Mrs. Frierson, Mama Maria, and many others.

That points out an important truth for every servant leader, both aspiring and established. There are helpful coaches around us all the time if we take the opportunity to look for them and, just as important, to appreciate what they can offer us.

THERE ARE HELPFUL COACHES AROUND US ALL THE TIME IF WE TAKE THE OPPORTUNITY TO LOOK FOR THEM AND, JUST AS IMPORTANT, TO APPRECIATE WHAT THEY CAN OFFER US.

Eventually, a developing servant leader becomes a coach to those around him or her. By looking to serve the people they lead, servant leaders are naturally offering coaching, guidance, direction, and other ways of developing personal growth and success.

That sets up what is to me a really interesting flow. On the one hand, servant leaders looking to improve their leadership skills can benefit by knowing what to look for in a coach—what abilities, attributes, and other talents a coach can share to help the servant leader grow.

Ultimately, though, that aspiring leader needs to take a different look at those skills—this time, in terms of what he or she can offer as a coach. It's very much like starting out in the role of a student who, over time, becomes an eager teacher.

In this chapter, I'll share with you what I've always looked for in any coach with whom I've worked—on the football field and beyond. By pointing out what I've found to be most valuable in a coach, I hope to guide you to look for similar skills and abilities in those potential coaches in your life.

From there, I'll talk about the role of a servant leader as a coach—how I've come to see my role as a servant leader and, in turn, specific strategies and ideas I use to be the most effective coach possible for those with whom I come into contact.

I owe so much of what I've become in my life to those coaches who invested their time and energy in me. I hope you have as much success in your journey as I have had in mine.

Before starting on any journey, it's essential to know your destination. With that in mind, when determining what to look for in a coach, first ask yourself: *What am I trying to achieve?*

On a simple level, goals can be fairly straightforward. For instance, in my role as a football player and quarterback, I always looked for a coach who would be able to take my skills to the next level. That was determined, in part, by where I happened to be as a player at that time. Was my passing accuracy a skill that needed work? Play calling? The ability to read a defense? No matter where I was in my development, I always looked at a coach through the lens of my goals at the time. I looked for what I knew I needed.

The same can apply to your situation. For example, in your profession, what skills do you need to develop to further your career? Do they have something specific to do with your job performance, or are those things more intangible, such as communication or other types of interpersonal skills? What you determine you need at the moment can impact the sort of person you might look to for coaching guidance.

That goes for your personal life as well. Are you happy with your home life, your family relationships, and your friendships? If you'd like to improve them, consider what you may be learning in your professional life. Many workplace lessons learned through a coach or mentor apply to your life outside of work.

Another skill I've always prioritized in any coach with whom I've worked is clarity of communication. This is a topic I cannot stress strongly enough. An effective coach needs to be a top-notch communicator—to be able to share experiences and insights in the clearest terms possible. To my mind, it's an absolute requirement. No great coach has ever lived who was incapable of getting a message across clearly and to the point.

> NO GREAT COACH HAS EVER LIVED WHO WAS INCAPABLE OF GETTING A MESSAGE ACROSS CLEARLY AND TO THE POINT.

When I made a mistake in either college or the pros, I was lucky to be working with coaches gifted at explaining where I made my mistake and, just as important, what I needed to learn from that mistake so it wouldn't happen again.

That wasn't just on the football field. I saw it in my academic life as well. My tutor at Clemson, Mama Maria, is one of the most blunt and straightforward people I've ever met. When I would call her trying to wriggle my way out of a study session, she made no bones about how important our work together was. No excuses, period. I benefitted from that sort of direct talk—even when it meant I had to haul my butt over to her office and get back to work. Her message was not open to interpretation in any way.

Part of being a great communicator is being a great listener—another aspect of great coaching. Accomplished coaches do much more than talk about what you should do and why; they also encourage feedback. Furthermore, they take that feedback to heart. Communication is a two-way street, and a good coach makes certain the traffic flows in both directions.

A great coach is also perceptive. Many people can be effective coaches when the issues involved are limited to the obvious. But a great coach is always able to read between the lines, to pick up on issues of significance that others might miss or overlook. Great coaches see more than everyone else sees. They're skilled at spotting nuances and subtle clues.

COMMUNICATION IS A TWO-WAY STREET, AND A GOOD COACH MAKES CERTAIN THE TRAFFIC FLOWS IN BOTH DIRECTIONS.

Taking that further, a perceptive coach knows that performance is about more than just mechanics. Attitude, emotions, experiences, and other factors play important roles as well. Perceptive coaches understand that coaching is anything but a skin-deep matter.

To that end, a coach who picks up on a problem will look for issues beyond just performance. That coach will ask if anything is on your mind, if there's anything troubling you, how things are at home. If you're in school, a perceptive coach will make certain to ask how your studies are progressing, how your social life is going. That coach will always be on the lookout for some subtle reason behind what you are doing.

Just as important, a perceptive coach will know when to pull back on asking these sorts of questions. We all know what it feels like when someone with the very best intentions asks us if anything's wrong, only to be told in no uncertain terms to get out of our face. A perceptive coach will not push the issue needlessly. If yours is a solid relationship, the coach will know that you'll eventually open up when you're ready to talk and will back off when it's clear they need to back off.

That goes hand in hand with another central attribute: honesty. Great coaches are honest without exception—with others and with themselves. They own up to their mistakes. By the same token, if they see something they feel a need to point out to you, they're just as honest in their willingness to do so.

Admittedly, this is a tough hill to climb. Let's face it, we've all been dishonest at one time or another. But honest coaches invariably will admit that, yes, they were short of being completely honest or forthright. In a way, it's the most powerful form of honesty there is—acknowledging to everyone that they're not flawless.

As I've mentioned in other parts of this book, I value a sense of balance—a mindset that keeps things in perspective. All of my best coaches have shared this attribute. Of course, they wanted me to succeed at whatever I was pursuing, but they also recognized that their work with me was just one part of my development as a person.

For instance, the football coaches I've been fortunate enough to play for have all been top-notch teachers of the sport—in strategy, technique, conditioning, and other aspects. But they've also recognized that the lessons learned in football aren't limited to the field; they're also a means to teach critical life lessons, such as teamwork, communication, and dedication. That was particularly important to me when I was a young player in high school and college just beginning to learn my craft. I began to understand the totality of the coaching I was receiving.

I also believe that the best coaches work with the entire person—not just the athlete, student, employee, or some other role that someone may occupy. They understand that everyone is made up of different talents, interests, and priorities. In keeping with a sense of perspective, they recognize that the particular skill or talent they happen to be addressing is no more or less important than any other part of a person's life. As I said, they coach the entire person, not just one part.

Coaches Miller and Perry back in high school were exceptional at this. And they had to be. Since they knew what my family and I were going through with my mom's cancer, they always took the time to ask how things at home were, how my mom was doing. Not only did they know that Mom's health would affect my on-field performance, but they also wanted to convey their interest in me as a person, not just a football talent. Like all gifted coaches, they understood that they couldn't possibly coach plays while ignoring the player.

> THE BEST COACHES WORK WITH THE ENTIRE PERSON—NOT JUST THE ATHLETE, STUDENT, EMPLOYEE, OR SOME OTHER ROLE THAT SOMEONE MAY OCCUPY. THEY UNDERSTAND THAT EVERYONE IS MADE UP OF DIFFERENT TALENTS, INTERESTS, AND PRIORITIES.

Leslie Frierson, one of my grade-school teachers back in Gainesville, is another ideal example of this. When I met NFL player Kendrick Lewis, she immediately picked up on how excited I was to interact with an actual professional football player. She knew I aspired to play professionally myself someday. She encouraged me to pursue that dream, but she was also thoughtful enough to remind me that my schoolwork would have to go hand in hand with my growth as a football player. That's the kind of perspective I'm talking about—not one that sees just a football player or just a student, but the entire person.

A coach who understands the importance of coaching the complete person recognizes that this approach leads to the very best results. Even young people know when a coach is treating them as a person rather than just a performer or player. As a result, they're motivated to work that much harder, and not just in one area of their lives. The complete person works that much more diligently at everything he or she is doing.

I believe great coaches are also selfless. Their goal in working with someone is not success for themselves—in effect, leveraging others for their own personal achievement (although, naturally enough, a great coach celebrates success). Rather, they're dedicated to the betterment of others, to always putting the interests of those around them ahead of their own.

Dabo Swinney at Clemson is just such a coach. I knew it from the earliest days of our relationship. After much thought and prayer, I decided to commit to Clemson early, well before the deadline when I had to formally make up my mind.

A coach who was solely concerned about the success of his football program would have done little more than, in effect, say: "Great. Just sign here."

Not Coach Swinney. He reminded me that I still had plenty of time to make such a critical decision, and he asked me if it wouldn't be better to wait a bit. Give it some more thought, more prayer. Make absolutely certain that this was the right choice for me.

His response only reaffirmed my decision that Clemson was, in fact, just the place for me. Even in high school, I could recognize his selflessness, his focus on the well-being of the person making the choice rather than how his own program and career might benefit. And, in the end, it was the best choice for me, thanks in large part to a coach who placed greater importance on my future than he did on what I might be able to contribute to his football team.

I also believe that great coaches are loyal without exception. They are loyal to the people they lead, to the program they represent, and to themselves. They understand that, if they cannot be loyal to themselves, then it's simply not possible to show meaningful loyalty toward anyone else.

Chad Morris epitomizes a coach who's loyal.

Coach Morris, who, as I write this, serves as the offensive coordinator and quarterback coach at Auburn University, was a central person in my life in a number of ways. Before eventually settling at Auburn, he was the head football coach at the University of Arkansas as well as Southern Methodist University, and, prior to all that, was the offensive coordinator at Clemson.

He was central in my decision to attend Clemson. Prior to my commitment, he was always there for me, answering questions and continually trying to assure me that Clemson would be just the place for me. In many ways, he complemented Coach Swinney's focus on making sure I made the right choice. In Coach Morris's mind, Clemson was the very best place for me to grow athletically, academically, and personally. As I've made clear, he was certainly right about that. He was loyal from the outset.

Coach Morris was also loyal to the program at Clemson. Prior to his arrival after the 2010 season, the offense had continually struggled, ranking eighty-sixth in scoring. Coach Morris was determined to improve on that dismal statistic by making things as simple as possible—play fast, play with focus, and put the ball in the hands of players with the best skills to make things happen. Simple and very effective.

From a football perspective, the rest is history, as they say.

But Coach Morris is much more than a gifted teacher. I could sense his loyalty and the bond that we had from the first time we spoke. Ultimately, I came to see him as a father figure, one whose loyalty can never be compromised. We talk on a regular basis to this day.

When he was hired at Arkansas, I let everyone know my feelings about Coach Morris via the media:

"Arkansas's got a great coach in Chad Morris. What I love about him most is he's a very loyal man. He's been there since Day 1 for me and been that father figure I never had in my life. He's very energetic, very truthful and very honest. He makes everyone around him better and has a bright future. Arkansas hired the right man to lead their football program. All love to the Morris family!"[1]

True to his loyal nature, Coach Morris has always been there to return the love.

"[Deshaun is] constantly in contact with me, he talks to (wife) Paula more than he does me," he was quoted saying on Jim Rome's radio program. "He talks to my two kids. He's like an older brother to my two kids. He's the type of kid your daughter brings home and says she wants to spend the rest of her life with a guy like him. Man, you would embrace that every day. He's that special of a person."[2]

Great coach; even greater, more loyal man.

Ultimately, great coaches are gifted life teachers. They understand that the lessons they're sharing go beyond what may occur on the field or the court. They recognize that something far more important than points being scored or games won or lost is taking place. By focusing their teaching on one particular aspect of your life—be it athletics, academics, or some other area—they know full well that growth is occurring within the entire person.

Those are just a sampling of some of the gifts that my coaches have given me over the years. There are many more, but I believe these are an excellent starting point to help you identify what you would value in a coach. For me, their value boiled down to a relatively simple question: *Is what they're sharing making me into a better, more complete person?* Over time I've amended this to include: *a more skilled and intuitive servant leader?*

> GREAT COACHES ARE GIFTED LIFE TEACHERS. THEY UNDERSTAND THAT THE LESSONS THEY'RE SHARING GO BEYOND WHAT MAY OCCUR ON THE FIELD OR THE COURT.

I'm now in a position to, in effect, return the favor by acting as a leader to those around me, both on the football field and elsewhere. Naturally, I've tried to develop the same kind of attributes I've embraced in my coaches. I've also been inspired to focus on additional skills that I feel are critical to being an effective servant leader.

Many of these attributes were also present in the coaches with whom I've worked. But I'm now seeing their value from the other side of the formula—as a servant leader looking to bring out the very best in everyone around me.

One thing I believe great servant leaders do is inspire those around them. Through their example, they boost others' energy level, commitment, and dedication to hard work. They help others believe they're capable of achieving greatness and of overcoming any obstacles or setbacks.

To be absolutely clear, that isn't a question of being some sort of cheerleader. Most people see through a lot of rah-rah nonsense—all talk, empty words. Instead, as I pointed out, a servant leader inspires others by example. Servant leaders share what they've achieved, not as a form of bragging but as an illustration of what's possible.

That's about more than just acknowledging what's happened in the past. For the servant leader, serving as an example is an ongoing, living entity. To coach others about the value of hard work and dedication, servant leaders look to make everything they do an illustration of hard work and dedication. If they coach about the value of listening, they work to develop their own listening skills to the utmost.

A coach and servant leader also works hard to support others. Support is made up of many of the qualities I've already pointed out, such as perception, balance, and great listening skills. Those and other attributes all contribute to a servant leader who is there when people need a lift. A great coach will certainly encourage you to learn from your mistakes but won't let you wallow in them.

> A GREAT COACH WILL CERTAINLY ENCOURAGE YOU TO LEARN FROM YOUR MISTAKES BUT WON'T LET YOU WALLOW IN THEM.

That doesn't mean servant leaders see everything through rose-colored glasses, that they never stop smiling no matter how challenging the situation. That isn't necessarily support; often, that's just kidding yourself. Instead, a skilled coach will maintain a realistic form of support—always looking to boost confidence and commitment without downplaying significant challenges and hurdles.

In the context of support, my friend Cam Newton has also served as a great coach for me. As I've mentioned before, he was there for me after the devastating loss in the national championship game to Alabama. Not only did he look to boost my spirits, but he also offered practical, powerful advice to help me keep moving forward. He was supportive but a realist. The world didn't end with the Alabama loss. As Cam supported me, he helped me understand that the game set the stage for all the work that remained to be done.

Great coaches are also realistic in other ways. They know what they have to work with and what they don't. This is perhaps one of their most overlooked traits. They're dedicated to working to help others grow and improve but, by the same token, they're not going to try to work with something that simply doesn't exist.

On the football field, I've seen what happens when some coaches have an unrealistic view of the skill of their team. For instance, I've seen teams try to emphasize a running game when they simply don't have the blocking up front. I've seen teams try to leverage a passing game with a subpar quarterback. That isn't constructive. Rather than trying to improve something that simply can't be improved very much, it's far better to address known strengths and work to make the most of those.

You may have seen this yourself in Pop Warner football, Little League, or school sports. Perhaps a coach's son or daughter has a role on a team that they're simply not equipped to handle. Maybe they get more playing time just because of the family ties. I'm all for giving people every opportunity to grow and succeed, but there has to be some sort of ability or experience there to start with. In many cases, leaders who make those types of decisions aren't truly giving others the chance to make good—they're merely setting them up for failure. A solid coach and servant leader knows the distinction between offering qualified people a realistic chance and placing less-qualified people way too close to the edge.

A great coach is not only confident but is also able to convey what confidence is and isn't. Confidence doesn't mean being some strutting braggart, always at the ready to crow about an achievement or success. To me, that only suggests a level of insecurity. If you have to talk about it, then it's possible you really don't believe it.

Instead, for me, confidence means a realistic understanding of what you can do—as well as those things that you may need others' help with. This comes back to the importance of balance. Confidence is a balanced view of yourself—what you're good at and what you need to work on.

Confidence also has to do with a desire to take on challenging situations and circumstances. If you're genuinely confident, you want to have to come back from a losing game. You want that challenge, that sense of obligation and responsibility.

> CONFIDENCE IS A BALANCED VIEW OF YOURSELF—WHAT YOU'RE GOOD AT AND WHAT YOU NEED TO WORK ON.

I remember hearing Michael Jordan say once that, when the game was on the line, he wanted the ball in his hands. He hungered to be in that position. Notice, too, what he didn't say. He didn't mention anything about wanting to take the last shot. Instead, he wanted the ball so he could position it for success—whether that meant him taking a shot or passing one off to a teammate. He wanted to have the ball so he could decide what move would work best. That's confidence.

Tom Brady is like that as well. In the most pressure-packed situations, he wants to be the quarterback involved in the play that decides everything. It's not a question of whether he's the one doing the scoring or not. He just wants to help a winning play happen, no matter who eventually crosses the goal line. For Tom, confidence isn't just a *me* thing, it's an *us* thing.

That illustrates another aspect of a coach's confidence—the ability to inspire confidence in others. And that confidence doesn't exist in a vacuum. A coach's confidence shouldn't be so encompassing as to make others feel unnecessary or irrelevant. Instead, a great coach looks to build confidence in others. By boosting the overall confidence of the group, the coach helps the players move in the same direction, certain that they're ready to meet any challenge or obstacle.

A gifted coach and servant leader also makes it a point to be constructively critical. Criticism and feedback are necessary components of a coach's overall responsibility, but they should never be delivered without a constructive slant. Pointing out mistakes for the sake of pointing out mistakes is easy; framing them in the context of a lesson is a completely different challenge.

In fact, that's one of the most significant tipping points between poor coaching and great coaching. Inexperienced or lazy coaches are prone to limiting feedback to simple criticism.

> CRITICISM AND FEEDBACK ARE NECESSARY COMPONENTS OF A COACH'S OVERALL RESPONSIBILITY, BUT THEY SHOULD NEVER BE DELIVERED WITHOUT A CONSTRUCTIVE SLANT.

On the other hand, gifted coaches won't pull any punches when discussing what went wrong, but they will make certain to take it further, offering ideas and suggestions for learning from a mistake and ways to improve. One approach just pushes people away; the other draws them closer.

That said, a true coach and servant leader knows when it's time to keep quiet. In many ways, that runs counter to the stereotypical view of coaches—continually talking, occasionally screaming, constantly animated. But good coaches recognize the importance of allowing others to process a teaching moment or come to their own conclusions. Not every leadership moment needs to be filled with chatter or commentary.

The very best coaches and servant leaders are flexible by nature. Of course, the more experienced they are, the more they'll know in advance what's going to work and what might not. But that doesn't cast strategy and teaching in stone—anything but. When others are having a hard time grasping what the coach is trying to get across, the last thing a good coach will do is fault them for an inability to "get it." Instead, the coach will approach their confusion as a teaching opportunity that calls for a different approach or some other alternative. That's not a case of lacking conviction; rather, it's a realistic acceptance of the situation and a willingness to change course in hopes of obtaining better results.

That means great coaches and servant leaders are constantly challenging themselves as much as the people around them. They understand that they're charged with learning and growing every bit as much as anyone else. Many gifted coaches treat every day as though it were their first on the job—they become blank slates, ready to benefit as much as they hope to serve others. Servant leaders and coaches approach challenges and opportunities as roads for growth for themselves and those around them.

———————

Great coaches also have terrific staying power. They display strength through longevity, a strength that allows them to continue to lead despite the adversity they will inevitably face.

GREAT COACHES AND SERVANT LEADERS ARE CONSTANTLY CHALLENGING THEMSELVES AS MUCH AS THE PEOPLE AROUND THEM. THEY UNDERSTAND THAT THEY'RE CHARGED WITH LEARNING AND GROWING EVERY BIT AS MUCH AS ANYONE ELSE.

That's why I think New Orleans quarterback Drew Brees has been a sort of coach for me.

On one level, his performance and statistics are off the charts. In nineteen seasons, Brees has done almost everything he possibly can and then some: he's won a Super Bowl, been a Super Bowl MVP, and been named to twelve Pro Bowls, and he holds several NFL all-time records. He has the respect of both teammates and opponents.

His longevity and consistency also inspire me. If you look at his record year in and out, there's a stunning level of consistency—four or five thousand yards passing almost every year. And considering all the physical punishment every quarterback has to deal with—as I write this, Brees is recovering from surgery on his throwing hand to repair a torn ligament—his is a remarkable example of dedication, durability, and the ability to rebound from setbacks.

But Brees is so much more than an amazing athlete. He's always been a guy I look up to. Every time I see him, we stop and talk. I always learn something of value from him. He's a great role model, a great family guy, and a great father. Anybody trying to be a quarterback at this level should look up to him as well.

He may never have won league MVP—a fact that never fails to blow me away—but, as a servant leader, he's a repeat winner.

My teammate J. J. Watt is another example of what I would call a more informal sort of coach.

For one thing, we both have very visible positions in the city of Houston. In addition to our time spent playing together, we've also done a fair amount of rehab work together. That's where I think J. J. serves as a coach: his determination, focus, and work ethic are all things you want to emulate.

But it's also J. J.'s role in the community—his work raising money for hurricane victims—that makes him an even more inspiring coach. He recognizes that being a celebrity also means taking on additional responsibility in helping others, particularly during challenging times. As a coach, he's helped me see that individuals blessed with a particular ability or standing in the community need to do more, and he never fails to do just that.

Ultimately, I think one of the most important characteristics of great coaches and servant leaders is their sense of gratitude. They never take their role for granted; they embrace it and the opportunity they've been given to influence others. It's also one of the most obvious traits to spot. A coach's attitude, approach, and dedication all underscore a strong sense of gratitude.

That's an example I've truly taken to heart. As a developing servant leader, I'm grateful every day for the position I'm in and the opportunity I've been given to make a genuine difference in the lives of most everyone I meet.

I have a long line of great coaches to thank for that—and, one day, you will as well.

PASS IT ON ━━━━━━━━━━━━━━━━━━━━━━━

- Think about the characteristics and attributes you value in a coach. Then list the people in your life who possess those characteristics. Can you add any others to make your coaching experience more complete?
- What does being confident mean to you? Where's the tipping point between confidence and arrogance? How do you inspire confidence in others? If someone is arrogant or overly confident, how can you as a leader bring that person back toward a more balanced sense of confidence?
- Think of someone you know who you consider a confident person. How does that person speak and act? Think about what makes the confidence admirable without dissolving into arrogance. Then think about how those attributes contribute to great leadership.

YOUR CHALLENGE

As a developing servant leader, list what skills you can offer others as a coach. Are there characteristics you think would be valuable to add? Who can you emulate to broaden your servant leadership by broadening your coaching skills?

A FEW NUMBERS LIT UP ON THE SCOREBOARD ARE JUST THAT—A FEW NUMBERS THAT TELL THE FINAL STORY BUT NOT HOW EVERYONE GOT THERE.

CHAPTER 12

REALITY AND FANTASY:
MY FAVORITE GAMES AND
MY PERFECT GAME

Every professional athlete embraces those special games or accomplishments—times when something magical occurs. Think of Franco Harris's "Immaculate Reception" or the New England Patriots' comeback from a twenty-five-point deficit in Super Bowl LI.

I've been part of those sorts of games. And, believe me, those are also all the games that everyone else remembers as well.

I've had people come up to me and rattle off stats from, say, the national championship title game against Alabama. Back in my hometown of Gainesville, some people can recite my high school's state championship game almost play by play.

As I said, those are the most visible types of games, and every athlete lives to experience them. I've been blessed to take part in a number of games that drew national, coast-to-coast attention.

But I also know that sort of attention, however rewarding in its own way, is not what leadership is all about. Many factors are far more important and valuable than people remembering final scores and statistics—things such as dedication, loyalty, trust, and any number of characteristics that servant leaders should have in their tool kit.

That's why I've decided to include this chapter of my favorite "under the radar" games—those games that meant a great deal to me but didn't get the attention of a national championship bowl game or an NFL playoff game.

Even though they may not have gotten the same level of attention as other games I've been in, I've found these games to be most instructive to me as a servant leader. In a certain way, it's as though less prominent games can be particularly educational; their lessons and message aren't as likely to be drowned out by mass attention, which can prove to be distracting.

I'll conclude this chapter with a description of my perfect game—my imaginary scenario of how an ideal game should go. It contains a few surprises you might not expect, particularly from the standpoint of development as a servant leader.

OCTOBER 1, 2017: TENNESSEE TITANS IN HOUSTON

I discussed this game briefly in an earlier part of the book, but to recap: we won at home 57–14. Personally, I completed twenty-five of thirty-four passes for 283 yards, four touchdowns, and one interception. I also rushed for 24 yards and one touchdown.

The game itself offered plenty to be proud of. My five total scores tied for the second-most touchdowns scored by a rookie in NFL history behind Gale Sayers's six touchdowns in 1965 (nice company). I also tied for the most touchdowns in a game by a rookie quarterback in NFL history. Not long thereafter, I was named AFC Offensive Player of the Week.

But it was meaningful in ways that went beyond statistics and honors.

For one thing, it was the first significant win in my professional career. It's true that we had already beaten Cincinnati earlier in the year, but that was a much closer game. This one was far more dominant.

Because I was a young player, the win was beneficial for me in a number of ways. First, it was a real confidence builder. I've always been a confident person by nature, but even the most self-assured among us occasionally needs evidence to support that attitude. The Titans game gave me that confidence boost. I knew for sure I could play very well at this level, and the win did a lot for my view of my skills.

It was also a very important game to me with regard to my leadership skills. This was my first professional game in which I played the entire time. In the huddle, I could sense the other players' confidence in me. Further, I could tell their own confidence was growing too. They knew as well as I did that this was no fluke. The growing group synergy was amazing to experience.

Perhaps most valuable of all, I recognized that, despite the success of a lopsided game, this was no time to rest on our laurels. Sure, the win was great,

> THE TITANS GAME GAVE ME THAT CONFIDENCE BOOST. I KNEW FOR SURE I COULD PLAY VERY WELL AT THIS LEVEL, AND THE WIN DID A LOT FOR MY VIEW OF MY SKILLS.

but we needed to keep our focus and continue to move forward. I made sure to share that sentiment with the rest of my teammates.

I was learning the servant leader's role in making certain that success doesn't lead to complacency. It was great to celebrate the win, but not everything about the game was 100 percent perfect. We needed to work on those lapses and mistakes to continue to enjoy success.

I was living the advice that Tom Brady once shared with me: always look at yourself as the underdog, the one with something to prove. Keeping that attitude in mind was a bit challenging given the big win, but I worked to sustain it. The last thing a servant leader wants to see is short-term success that compromises long-term objectives. I did not want that to happen, and I continue to keep that mindset to this day.

PASS IT ON

- Think back to a time or experience when you enjoyed great success. How long did you allow yourself to bask in the glow of that success? Did it lead to issues later on, such as complacency? Or did that success fuel your hunger to keep working as hard as possible?

YOUR CHALLENGE

The next time you're successful at something, look at yourself as the underdog—one for whom that sort of success is somewhat surprising. Maintain that underdog attitude as you move forward, and see if it leads to continued success. Remember that the underdog is always the hungriest one in the pack.

OCTOBER 29, 2017: SEATTLE SEAHAWKS IN SEATTLE

This was a wild game, to put it mildly. The final result, a 41–38 loss to the Seahawks, doesn't paint the entire picture that the game deserves. It careened back and forth the entire way. We were tied 21–21 at the end of the first half, and Seattle inched ahead three points by the end of the third quarter.

Then things really burst loose. We scored two touchdowns in the final quarter to inch out a four-point lead. But Russell Wilson, the Seahawks' dominant quarterback and leader, was on the other side of the ball.

Down 38–34 with 1:39 left and no timeouts remaining, Wilson took Seattle eighty yards in barely a minute. He hit Paul Richardson for forty-eight yards on a jump ball to start the drive and found Tyler Lockett for nineteen more yards. He then zipped a strike to Jimmy Graham for the game winner. I wasn't able to respond and was intercepted by Richard Sherman on a desperation throw with seven seconds left.

Again, the numbers were great—for the most part. I threw for 402 yards and four touchdowns. At that point in the season, I had nineteen passing touchdowns, the most by a rookie in his first seven games of a season.

But I was also intercepted three times, twice by Sherman—a continuing issue I needed to work on. Even worse, one of the interceptions by Earl Thomas was returned seventy-eight yards for a pick-six touchdown.

Still, the Seahawks were very complimentary of our team and of me. In fact, Wilson joked at the end of the game that the league should "go ahead and give him rookie of the year. I love watching him."[1]

But the pleasure was every bit as much mine in watching Wilson work. His athletic ability goes without saying. He finished twenty-six of forty-one passes for a career-high 452 yards and four touchdowns.

But the intangibles were also off the charts. His poise, his ability to make intelligent decisions on the fly, and his competitiveness shone through on every play. You could see that Russell never takes a play off, no matter if the Seahawks are winning by five touchdowns or down twenty-eight with a minute to go.

That was a great lesson for me as a servant leader. In watching Wilson perform, it was obvious how hard he constantly worked, how he never let his energy level lag for an instant. Moreover, I could see how he shared that energy with the rest of his teammates, raising their game.

It was also a lesson that a servant leader cannot live in a vacuum. By that I mean, no matter how successful an individual servant leader may be, success means very little if the group as a whole doesn't also enjoy a similar level of success. In this case, both Wilson and I turned in great individual performances. In his case, however, that success was tied into the success of the team. To me, that matters more than the most amazing individual statistic imaginable.

NO MATTER HOW SUCCESSFUL AN INDIVIDUAL SERVANT LEADER MAY BE, SUCCESS MEANS VERY LITTLE IF THE GROUP AS A WHOLE DOESN'T ALSO ENJOY A SIMILAR LEVEL OF SUCCESS.

This game also reinforced the teaching value of failure. As I've stressed, losing can teach you far more than winning can. It's important to approach a loss as a learning experience every bit as much as a disappointment—hopefully a short-lived disappointment.

PASS IT ON ══════════════════════════

- Consider an experience where you or someone else enjoyed amazing individual success but the group as a whole did not. If that was you, how did it make you feel? If it was someone else, how did that person react? Did he or she crow about the achievement or express more concern about the others who were not as successful?

YOUR CHALLENGE

Approach your next group project or challenge with two-tiered attention. Pay attention to both your own personal success and that of the entire group. Are they similar levels of success? If you're more successful than the others, examine your behavior—are you more happy or disappointed? Consider if you as a servant leader can sacrifice some of your own personal success so that the group as a whole benefits.

DECEMBER 25, 2017: PITTSBURGH STEELERS IN HOUSTON

This may seem like an unusual choice to be included in meaningful games.

For one thing, it took place on Christmas Day. As much as I love playing football, because I'm a Christian, this day obviously has a good deal more meaning to me than just another game day.

For another, it was a blowout. The Steelers manhandled us from the opening kickoff to the final whistle, 34–6. They took a quick ten-point lead in the first quarter capped by a touchdown pass from Ben Roethlisberger to Justin Hunter and never looked back from there. Our only score came in the fourth quarter on a touchdown throw to DeAndre Hopkins. It was pretty much a one-sided affair from beginning to end.

Perhaps even more unusual, it wasn't me who made that touchdown pass; it was T. J. Yates. I didn't play a single down in this game.

It was several weeks after my season-ending ACL tear. I watched from the sidelines in frustration—over the way the game went as well as my inability to do anything about it.

That's why I've included this particular game in my list of meaningful NFL experiences. This one taught me a number of valuable lessons.

First, participation is everything. Lacking any way of contributing to the effort of the group is one of the most frustrating ordeals a servant leader can experience. If you're hoping to lead, being removed from what's going on can be an exercise in futility.

But even though I was upset about not being able to play, I realized that I had to contribute in any way possible, no matter what that might be. In my case, I talked to T. J. as much as I could, offering my perspective as to what he might try the next time we had the ball. As a servant leader, even if you don't occupy the role you would like to, at the very least you can look for ways to continue to lead and support those around you.

That game reinforced my conviction to regain my physical health and return to playing shape as soon as I could. Anger and helplessness can be powerful motivators, and I experienced both those emotions on that Christmas Day. I knew I had to get back to where I needed to be and where the team needed me to be. It really honed my focus.

That game also reinforced my desire to learn as much as possible, no matter the circumstances. For me, that meant studying Ben Roethlisberger as much as I could, watching him direct Pittsburgh's offense and taking mental notes of how he went through his progressions to find an open receiver. As I've said before, a growing servant leader is always a student, and I tried to take as much away from that game as possible, knowing I could use the information to my benefit later.

> THAT GAME REINFORCED MY CONVICTION TO REGAIN MY PHYSICAL HEALTH AND RETURN TO PLAYING SHAPE AS SOON AS I COULD.

And it was a game we lost. Again, losing is always a far better teacher than winning. When you win, it's easy to get caught up in all the things you did right without paying enough attention to things that demand work—and there are always things to be worked on. When you lose, everything is called into question, and rightfully so. You always lose for a reason— usually, several reasons—and it challenges you to step up and honestly review what happened. Losing is a call to action to improve that you can't ignore.

Lastly, the game was yet another education in patience. First, I couldn't play, which required acceptance on my part. Second, we lost—a challenge to review just what went wrong that also mandated patience.

Additionally, the timing of the game was a valuable lesson in patience that cuts both ways. On the one hand, we were nearing the end of the season. There was just one more game on the schedule—and with a 4–11 record at the time, the only place we were going after the last game was home. We were struggling. There weren't going to be any more "next weeks" to look forward to for a while. There were no short-term opportunities at redemption on the horizon.

But in my case as well as the entire team's, the fact that the season was ending—with many months to go before we stepped on a field to play a meaningful game again—afforded the opportunity of time. For me, I had the time to rehab and get back into playing shape. For the team, there was time to review what had happened during a disappointing season, make adjustments, and, hopefully, perform much better when the next season arrived.

Patience, I came to learn, is one of the most important tools in a servant leader's skill set. Leaders can take a period of time that others might see as long and frustrating and, instead, make the most of the opportunity that time affords to learn, grow, and improve—and point out that opportunity to the others they wish to serve.

PASS IT ON

- When was the last time you experienced a loss or some other form of disappointment and could do nothing about it? How did it make you feel? Did you see yourself as completely helpless, or did you do what you could under whatever circumstances you encountered?

YOUR CHALLENGE

You can't be directly involved in every situation that means something to you. The next time that happens, look for any opportunity to contribute in some way or another. However small or seemingly insignificant, look to see how your contribution impacts what's going on. You may be pleasantly surprised by the results of what you thought would be of little value.

MY PERFECT GAME

Now, having covered some real-life examples, let's talk about what I would consider my perfect game—not necessarily the best in terms of outcome but in terms of what would occur during the game itself and what the competitors would derive from the experience.

The term *perfect game* generally suggests something, well, perfect. Something without any mistakes or mishaps. In baseball, for instance, a perfect game means no hits, no runs, and not even a single base runner.

People often ask me if I think I've ever played a perfect game. The reply is an obvious no. Regardless of the outcome of the game, no matter how fantastic the statistics, I've never played a perfect game. There's always room for improvement.

But as a servant leader looking for every opportunity to grow and improve, I've thought a lot about what a perfect game would be like from my perspective. What sort of game would be most valuable to me in terms of what I could take away and learn from the experience?

Here's what I would consider a perfect game. Some of the details and characteristics may surprise you!

First, the teams would be evenly matched, down to the very last player on the bench, the coaching staff, the medical support people, the temperature of the Gatorade, everything. Breaking it down mathematically, that would mean that both teams would have a completely equal chance of winning.

Obviously, in the real world, that's simply not possible. No two teams have ever competed on a completely equal footing. I always have to chuckle a bit when I hear or read something about two teams being evenly matched. There's really no such thing. They may be close in ability, perhaps, but never completely even.

But, in my mind, a perfect game would naturally involve two teams that are mirror images of each other. That would offer the best opportunity for each team to showcase their abilities, strategy, and execution. The challenge would be balanced—something a servant leader embraces.

(This may seem to run counter to the advice Tom Brady gave me about always looking at yourself as the underdog. It doesn't; that's a mindset, not necessarily a fact. Looking at yourself as the underdog is a form of motivation—something to draw from when you're in an evenly matched situation.)

Further, a perfect game for me would have plenty of mistakes in addition to incredible performances. Again, that may seem to contradict the very idea of a perfect game. Like the baseball pitcher who completely shuts down the opposition, you would think any "perfect game" would be utterly flawless.

But the perfect game that exists only in my mind would have its share of mistakes. And the reason should be obvious by now—mistakes are among our very best teachers, as long as you let them take on that role. Being mistake-free is not only impossible but it denies us the chance to experience mistakes for what they are: opportunities for growth and improvement.

That's why, in my perfect game, any mistake would happen only once. Whoever made a mistake would learn from it and never make it a second time.

There would still be injuries—though nothing serious! Injuries are just a form of setback, a challenge to be addressed and overcome. Servant leaders expect those sorts of hurdles and are able to adjust to whatever situation may arise. They also encourage others to anticipate similar setbacks.

Of course, the perfect game would include any number of amazing plays. But it's important to break down what that entails. On the one hand, an amazing play might be the result of perfect execution—a carefully mapped-out plan that goes off without a hitch. But an amazing play might also include improvisation—one in which the plan breaks down yet something remarkable takes place.

If you think about it, that mirrors real life. Sometimes success happens as the result of following a carefully orchestrated road map. Other times success results from more of a mad scramble, an action or decision made on the fly. A servant leader recognizes that success can come by way of any number of paths—both mapped out and otherwise—and looks for opportunity everywhere.

This comes back to a point I raised earlier about how practice leads to great improvisation. Of course, improvisation can happen after a play really goes wrong, but more often than not, great plays that seem to come out of nowhere happen because great execution got the players to that point. Knowing your stuff and going out and doing it position you to let instinct and natural ability take over.

A perfect game would go back and forth in terms of which team was enjoying the most success. That's the most instructive sort of flow. The perfect game shouldn't be all winning nor should it be all losing. The give-and-take that characterizes most everything in life should happen within a perfect game. It's the type of experience that teaches us the most—about ourselves, the opportunities and challenges we all have to confront, and how to work with others to obtain the best results.

THE GIVE-AND-TAKE THAT CHARACTERIZES MOST EVERYTHING IN LIFE SHOULD HAPPEN WITHIN A PERFECT GAME.

One part of my imagined perfect game does, in fact, happen in most real-life contests. Success would be celebrated, but only for a short time. Participants in the perfect game would understand that there's more game to be played and wouldn't wallow in success too long. There's always work that remains to be done.

As I said, this happens all the time in actual games. Players celebrate but then get right back to business. Take note of it the next time you watch a game. If any one player celebrates for too long, there's likely going to be someone nearby ready to help him or her regain focus and move forward.

So, here comes the ultimate question: Who wins the perfect game?

From my view, it really doesn't matter.

That may seem like a ridiculous thing for someone so competitive and focused on winning to suggest, but, in the case of a perfect game, it's true. That's because no matter the outcome, a perfect game would treat every participant as a student with different lessons to be learned—all of which are valuable.

For the winners, there's the joy in celebrating a successful effort, one to which every player has contributed. There's both satisfaction and a sense of confidence about reaching a goal. There's the opportunity for further success.

But winning shouldn't be all happiness and good times. Servant leaders are quick to remind others that they need to learn from whatever mistakes they may have made so they can overcome challenges and hurdles in the future. Success is wonderful, but there are goals and opportunities around the corner that demand attention and preparation.

So, too, is losing not exclusively all bad news. Granted, no one likes to lose, to come up short. None of us competes in order to lose. But, again, losing is a generous and dedicated teacher. It forces you to look at yourself as objectively as you can, identify what went wrong, and, from there, take practical steps to ensure that it doesn't happen again. It's a cruel but effective education.

That's why I say that the final score of my perfect game is irrelevant. Servant leaders are much more interested in what they gained from the experience, not to mention what others learned. A few numbers lit up on the scoreboard are just that—a few numbers that tell the final story but not how everyone got there.

And the journey is what matters to a servant leader.

PASS IT ON

- Have you ever been involved in an event or experience that came close to being perfect? What made it so special? What did you learn from the experience? Was there something about the situation that you could use in the future?

YOUR CHALLENGE

Map out your perfect game. The setting can be anywhere you want it to be—at home, school, work, wherever you like. Think carefully about every aspect that would, in fact, make your game perfect. Watch for both positives and negatives. Then apply what you've learned to an upcoming situation or challenge. See what you can do to make the experience as close to perfect as you can.

WHETHER WE RECOGNIZE IT—OR, FOR THAT MATTER, EVEN DESIRE IT—EACH AND EVERY ONE OF US IS A LEADER IN SOME CAPACITY.

CHAPTER 13

"BE LEGENDARY"

As I write this, the 2019–20 season is well underway—another football journey that's bound to be filled with triumphs as well as disappointments and setbacks.

I'm certain it's also going to be characterized by just as many lessons and experiences to further my development as a servant leader.

I'm particularly excited about it for a number of reasons. This marked one of the few off-seasons I've experienced throughout my playing career when I was completely healthy. As a result, I've come to learn about and appreciate a new level of dedication—one of the bedrocks of a successful servant leader.

My sole focus in the summer of 2019 was working to improve my craft, mentally and physically. The absence of any sort of physical recovery has allowed for greater focus on looking forward—on building rather than also having to rebuild at the same time.

THE ABSENCE OF ANY SORT OF PHYSICAL RECOVERY HAS ALLOWED FOR GREATER FOCUS ON LOOKING FORWARD—ON BUILDING RATHER THAN ALSO HAVING TO REBUILD AT THE SAME TIME.

It's also given me a completely fresh perspective on dedication—one that, strangely enough, suggests that success, however desirable, can undermine even the most committed of us.

My rookie year was straightforward with regard to dedication. I was new, and the team and the city of Houston expected a lot from me. Excitement was everywhere. In that sort of environment, dedication can come rather easily. With so much riding on who you are and what you do, it's easy to feed off all that energy.

After the injury that ended my first season, I was determined to come back in as optimal physical shape as possible. Again, dedication wasn't much of a hill to climb. When you've suffered a setback and are determined to get back on track, dedication is an absolute necessity. Without it, you'll likely be doing little more than spinning your wheels.

Of course, the start of every season has a vibe to it that stirs dedication. Since I had a solid second season last year and helped the team to the playoffs, it's natural that my teammates, fans, and the organization expect things to improve even more in the coming year. That can provide plenty of energy and focus.

But the off-season between my second and third years has been a barometer of my capacity to practice dedication. It's as though, lacking issues such as injury or the excitement of being the new face in town, dedication is all the more important—yet more of a challenge to maintain.

In the case of the Texans in 2019–20, dedication means taking the next step in the development of the overall team. Yes, we're defending AFC South Champions, but in the spirit of Tom Brady's suggestion, my teammates and I are refusing to compromise our dedication based on any sort of past success.

As a developing servant leader, I look to convey my sense of dedication to my teammates, as they do to me. Dedication involves a great deal of synergy. It's easy to pick out a team or some other group for whom dedication is a shared value as opposed to it being limited to just a few people. The more pervasive the dedication, the greater the results.

In my case, part of my overall dedication has to do with longevity. If all goes well and I stay reasonably healthy, I'd like to continue playing football until the age of forty, maybe even longer. With role models such as Brady (who, as of this writing, is forty-two years old) and Brees (forty, with a nineteen-year NFL career under his belt), I know it's far from an impossibility.

But that's a long way off.

> IF ALL GOES WELL AND I STAY REASONABLY HEALTHY, I'D LIKE TO CONTINUE PLAYING FOOTBALL UNTIL THE AGE OF FORTY, MAYBE EVEN LONGER.

At the outset of this book, I raised the issue of my age in terms of discussing servant leadership. I can appreciate why some readers—at least initially—may have had questions or doubts about a twenty-four-year-old sharing what he considers valuable lessons about ways to make your life more fulfilling and rewarding.

I grant you that I have much more to learn. But my situation represents a basic truth having to do with all servant leaders—we never stop learning about ways to make ourselves better and more dedicated leaders.

Even though I'm still relatively young, I feel I have experienced quite a bit in what amounts to just short of a quarter century. Growing up in poverty without a father, my mom's struggle with cancer, obtaining my college degree in only three years, and moving on to play professional football have packed a lot of joy and hardship into a rather brief amount of time.

I know that many of you have also experienced many joys, sorrows, triumphs, and tragedies in your own lives—maybe not in as condensed a timeline as I did, but still a lot of water under the bridge. No matter the particulars of your situation, I hope what I've shared has been entertaining but, just as important, instructional and inspirational in your growth as a servant leader.

Whether we recognize it—or, for that matter, even desire it—each and every one of us is a servant leader in some capacity.

That's because most things in life involve a group of some sort—a team, a family, a company, you name it. And although each of those groups may have a designated "leader," each of us at one time or another is called on to lead others. It can be something as simple as offering advice or feedback, but a form of leadership is always in play.

EACH OF US AT ONE TIME OR ANOTHER IS CALLED ON TO LEAD OTHERS.

We're called on to serve others in many additional ways. Again, that can fly under the radar to a certain extent, but interacting with others naturally involves some form of service. It can be obvious, such as helping a friend or loved one during a time of hardship or challenge or even something as quick and innocent as holding the door open for someone else, but some type of service is always taking place. Take the time to watch for these moments of service, and you may be surprised by how often we are all serving others.

That's one of the reasons I wrote this book. In many ways, people who identify with servant leadership and are actively working to develop their emotional and intellectual skills are aware of the constant nature of servant leadership. They're the easy part of the audience to talk to!

It's those who don't see themselves as servant leaders that I hope this book truly touches. As I've discussed, the benefits of servant leadership aren't limited just to the people who look to such leaders. Servant leaders mature and grow as people, too, rewarding themselves as well as those around them. They become more complete in all sorts of ways.

So, that begs the question: Just how do I anticipate my own continued growth as a servant leader to play out?

For me, that breaks down into a number of different goals.

First, like any professional athlete, I want to stand at the top of the pack. That means eventually capturing a Super Bowl championship. In looking at my own development as a player as well as the development of my teammates, the coaching staff, and the entire Texans organization, I am very confident that goal will be reached one day. Hopefully, that's sooner rather than later, but I recognize the value of patience in achieving goals of that magnitude.

Another goal is keeping my love for what I do amid the heat and emotions of chasing that dream. It may sound corny, but I absolutely love playing football, from the competition itself to the interaction with teammates and opponents to the game's constant challenge of both my physical and mental skills. By continuing to grow, I feel confident that the love and fire in my belly will continue to burn brightly.

Through my work and activities both on and off the football field, I also hope to continue to inspire others around me. Away from football, I know in my heart that one part of that will be continued involvement with Habitat for Humanity. Having not only experienced the personal joy that such a program can foster but also seeing that joy in others, I recognize that Habitat will remain a part of my life forever. Hopefully, as I continue to grow as a servant leader, I can bring even more to the organization. It's already given me more than I can possibly repay. I hope my foundation furthers that effort.

In pursuing these and other aspects of servant leadership, I hope to remain as relatable as possible to everyone with whom I come into contact. In its own way, staying grounded is as great a challenge as any other. For anyone with a conspicuous position in the public eye—be that an athlete, government official, performer, or something else—being relatable carries more meaning than you might assume at first.

> I HOPE TO REMAIN AS RELATABLE AS POSSIBLE TO EVERYONE WITH WHOM I COME INTO CONTACT. IN ITS OWN WAY, STAYING GROUNDED IS AS GREAT A CHALLENGE AS ANY OTHER.

On the one hand, remaining relatable means maintaining genuine connections with others. Sometimes success can be its own worst enemy in terms of your relationships with people. You may not see others in quite the same way or take as much time as you once did to understand and empathize with others. They seem distant.

A servant leader works diligently to make certain that doesn't happen. By developing and using many of the traits and attributes I've described in this book—humility, kindness, and a willingness for self-sacrifice, in addition to others—a servant leader never keeps anyone at arm's length. The very nature of servant leadership requires close, genuine connections. I hope my every action contributes to those connections.

But, just as important, a servant leader remains relatable to him- or herself. By that I mean never forgetting where you came from and the defining roles of your character and personality that cannot be changed. It's a commitment to never losing sight of what has made you who you are. Whether you keep contact through something you can see—such as writing "815" on your wristband before every game—or the beliefs you hold, you never have to look in a mirror one day and wonder who the person looking back at you truly is.

> THE VERY NATURE OF SERVANT LEADERSHIP REQUIRES CLOSE, GENUINE CONNECTIONS.

I urge you to use the exercises I've included at the end of each chapter to help you achieve that and other meaningful goals in your journey of servant leadership. Revisit them over time and gauge your progress. I'm confident that you'll be both pleased with the results and that much more committed to moving forward in your journey.

You may have found some of the issues and ideas contained in this book particularly helpful or applicable to your personal situation—the importance of remaining humble, for instance, or always treating yourself as the underdog when it comes to a challenge. But, above all, I encourage you to look for the leadership opportunities that are around you all the time—at work, at home, in school, wherever you happen to be. I hope this book has raised your awareness of the many ways you can grow while helping those around you to grow as well.

So, at the risk of repeating myself, let's all go be legendary.

PASS IT ON

- Take some time to think about what you consider the most valuable leadership message in this book. Dedication? The ability to bend but not break? Coming to understand that timing can be so important in choosing the right moments to lead?

YOUR CHALLENGE

Once you've identified that leadership quality you've learned more about in this book, share it with someone close to you. Think carefully about what to share and how you do so. As the title of this book suggests, we all have something, and we can pass it on to others.

NOTES

CHAPTER 6: NEVER GET TOO HIGH, NEVER SINK TOO LOW

1. John McClain (@McClain_on_NFL), Twitter, July 28, 2017, 9:33 a.m., https://twitter.com/mcclain_on_nfl/status/890943238848303104.
2. J. J. Watt (@JJWatt), Twitter, November 2, 2017, 5:08 p.m., https://twitter.com/JJWatt/status/926209339345592321.

CHAPTER 7: IGNORE THE DOUBTERS, FORGIVE THE HATERS

1. Dale Robertson, "Texans No Match for Colts in Playoff Loss," *Houston Chronicle*, January 6, 2019, https://www.chron.com/sports/texans/article/Houston-Texans-Indianapolis-Colts-playoffs-recap-13509719.php.
2. Julian Gill, "Onalaska ISD Superintendent Regrets Posting 'You Can't Count on a Black Quarterback,'" *Houston Chronicle*, September 19, 2018, https://www.chron.com/news/houston-texas/houston/article/Onalaska-ISD-superintendent-apologizes-for-13236285.php.
3. Gill, "Onalaska ISD Superintendent."

CHAPTER 9: NEVER STOP PRACTICING, NEVER STOP LEARNING

1. Ira Berkow, "Bird Shoots for Coaching Greatness with the Pacers," *New York Times*, August 10, 1997, https://www.nytimes.com/1997/08/10/sports/bird-shoots-for-coaching-greatness-with-the-pacers.html.
2. John McClain (@McClain_on_NFL), Twitter, June 21, 2017, 11:08 a.m., https://twitter.com/mcclain_on_nfl/status/877558780455772164.

3. Deshaun Watson (@deshaunwatson), Twitter, June 22, 2017, 10:08 a.m., https://twitter.com/deshaunwatson/status/877906199856857088.

4. Tyler Dunne, "Deshaun Watson Has No Off Switch," *Bleacher Report*, October 17, 2019, https://bleacherreport.com/articles/2858342-deshaun -watson-has-no-off-switch.

CHAPTER 11: FIND A COACH, BE A COACH

1. Bob Holt, Matt Jones, Tom Murphy, "Kudos Spread Wide for New UA Football Coach; Offense, Man Draw Plaudits," *Arkansas Democrat Gazette*, December 7, 2017, https://www.arkansasonline.com/news /2017/dec/07/kudos-spread-wide-20171207/.

2. "KJ Jefferson Shows Love for Deshaun Watson & Morris Family," *Best of Arkansas Sports* blog, December 3, 2018, http://www.bestofarkansassports .com/kj-jefferson-shows-love-for-deshaun-watson-morris-family/.

CHAPTER 12: REALITY AND FANTASY: MY FAVORITE GAMES AND MY PERFECT GAMES

1. AP, "Wilson's Heroics Lead Seahawks to Wild 41–38 Win over Texans," CBS Sports, October 30, 2017, https://www.cbssports.com/nfl/news /wilsons-heroics-lead-seahawks-to-wild-41–38-win-over-texans/amp/.

ABOUT THE AUTHORS

Deshaun Watson is quarterback for the Houston Texans and a former college All-American at Clemson University. While at Clemson, he led his team to the national championship game in 2015 and a national championship title in 2016. He was born in Gainesville, Georgia, and was a first-round draft pick to the NFL in 2017.

Lavaille Lavette is a bestselling author and editor of numerous books, including *New York Times* bestsellers. With a master's in education, Lavaille has worked as an investment broker, schoolteacher, school district administrator, speechwriter, and marketing executive, and she has served as special advisor to former U.S. Secretary of Education Rod Paige. Currently, Lavaille is president and publisher of two imprints, One Street Books and Ebony Magazine Publishing, in partnership with HarperCollins Publishers.